Praise for
How to Make Peace in the Middle East in Six Months or Less Without Leaving Your Apartment

"Gregory Levey may or may not be able to save the world. But I do know this: He writes a very entertaining and informative book. The section on Second Life alone is worth the price of admission."

—A. J. Jacobs, author of *My Life as an Experiment*

"Greg Levey has made a comic masterpiece out of the world's most intractable conflict—yet hidden among the sidesplitting laugh lines are insights about the Middle East that are no laughing matter. I've read dense scholarship on Israeli-Palestinian affairs that does not capture the irony or the humanity of the situation half as well as this hilarious book."

—Joseph Braude, author of *The New Iraq:*
Rebuilding the Country for Its People,
the Middle East, and the World

"The conflict in the Mideast isn't best handled by diplomats, ideologues, or think-tank wonks, but by Greg Levey, the one man with the courage to call it like it is: an exhausting, frustrating, dinner-party-killing morass, ruled over by nutjobs of all stripes. *HTMPITMEISMOLWLYA* is the comedic Oslo Plan we've been waiting for, and Levey delivers his diagnosis of the situation with the on-the-ground wisdom of Thomas Friedman and the experimental wit of A. J. Jacobs. Make laughs, not war."

—David Sax, author of *Save the Deli*

"Laughs AND insight—a killer combo. Loved it so much I am looking forward to 'How to Create Cold Fusion Without Getting Out of the Hot Tub.'"

—Lenore Skenazy, author of *Free-Range Kids*

"A lively and humorous account of one man's quest to solve the Israeli-Palestinian conflict. Levey's thoughtfulness and wit make this book an absorbing read for Middle East neophytes and veterans alike."

—Jennifer Miller, author of *Inheriting the Holy Land: An American's Search for Hope in the Middle East* *f*P

Also by Gregory Levey

Shut Up, I'm Talking: And Other Diplomacy Lessons
I Learned in the Israeli Government—A Memoir

How to MAKE PEACE
in the MIDDLE EAST
in SIX MONTHS
or LESS
Without LEAVING
Your APARTMENT

GREGORY LEVEY

FREE PRESS
New York   London   Toronto   Sydney

FREE PRESS
A Division of Simon & Schuster, Inc.
1230 Avenue of the Americas
New York, NY 10020

First Free Press hardcover edition September 2010

FREE PRESS and colophon are trademarks of Simon & Schuster, Inc.

For information about special discounts for bulk purchases,
please contact Simon & Schuster Special Sales at 1-866-506-1949
or business@simonandschuster.com.

The Simon & Schuster Speakers Bureau can bring authors to your live event.
For more information or to book an event contact the Simon & Schuster Speakers Bureau
at 1-866-248-3049 or visit our website at www.simonspeakers.com.

DESIGNED BY ERICH HOBBING

Manufactured in the United States of America

1   3   5   7   9   10   8   6   4   2

Library of Congress Cataloging-in-Publication Data
Levey, Gregory.
How to make peace in the Middle East in six months or less
without leaving your apartment / Gregory Levey.
p. cm.
Includes index.
1. Arab-Israeli conflict—1993—Peace. 2. United States—Relations—Israel. 3. Israel—
Relations—United States. 4. Levey, Gregory. 5. Jews—United States—Biography. I. Title.
DS119.76.L473 2010
956.05'4—dc22   2010005547

ISBN 978-1-4391-5415-1
ISBN 978-1-4391-6329-0 (ebook)

For my parents—
one a warrior,
the other a diplomat

I hope that someday we will be able to put away our fears and prejudices and just laugh at people.

—Jack Handey

Contents

Author's Note

I don't want to give anything away, so I'm not going to tell you whether or not I succeeded in making peace in the Middle East. You'll have to read this whole book if you want to find that out.

But I will tell you that my intention was never to make light of the tragic situation in the region. On the contrary, as I wrote in my first book, "Sometimes it is the comic details that best reflect the gravity of the larger picture."

To the best of my recollection, all the events recounted here are true. I really did play phone tag with the White House, go undercover as an Evangelical Christian, do combat training with a paramilitary group, and end up at a real castle owned by a guy who seemed to always wear a cape. But while I was quite often taking notes, for some events and conversations I have had to rely on memory, with its considerable limitations.

I have sometimes obscured people's personal details to protect their privacy. Astute readers, news junkies, and friends might notice that I have also tinkered with the chronology of events, both political and personal, and that in a few isolated cases, I have used composite characters. I did this to maintain narrative flow and in order to entertain you—so I don't want to hear any complaints about it. Don't be a Fundamentalist.

One final note. In looking over this book, it occurs to me that even if I intended to take a bird's-eye look at the Middle East situation, I have inevitably approached it from the point of view of someone who is North American, who is of my generation, who is secular, and who is Jewish. In other words, from my own perspective.

But with a conflict so dense and complicated, I think that's all any of us can hope to do.

—G.L., January 2010

How to MAKE PEACE
in the MIDDLE EAST
in SIX MONTHS
or LESS
Without LEAVING
Your APARTMENT

CHAPTER ONE

My Struggles with Dementia

I was in the hallway outside an auditorium, waiting to give a talk to the audience sitting inside, when the organizer of the event told me something that gave me cause for concern.

"Just so you know," she said, "your opening act has dementia."

I thought I must have misheard, and wanted to ask her to repeat herself, but she had already walked into the room to get things started.

My opening act has dementia? I thought. *What?*

To be honest, I was surprised to hear that I even had an opening act, since I was just a first-time author doing a talk about my book.

I stood just outside the room and watched a man in his early sixties take the podium and proceed to give a presentation that was part lecture about the Middle East, part prayer, and mostly gibberish. The audience, which was composed largely of middle-aged and elderly people, took it in stride, and later on I found out that this was the group's standard procedure. This guy was apparently a regular at these events and had a habit of yelling out nonsensical statements during people's presentations, so the thinking was that if they let him do his little talk before the real guest speaker went up, he was less likely to interrupt. Indeed, when he was finished, my opening act got a fair amount of applause. I took this as a good sign. Apparently I was dealing with an easy crowd.

That was the first time I had encountered literal dementia on my book tour, but because the book I was promoting was about the Middle East, more than a few of the people I was interacting with were a bit off the rails. I had encountered everything from armchair extremists more fanatical than their on-the-ground equivalents to peace activists so strident in their pacifism that they seemed on the verge of violence. In fact, these bizarre, often frustrating interactions had driven me to set a new goal for myself.

Mostly because I was tired of hearing about it, I had decided that I was going to personally solve the Middle East conflict.

The situation in the Middle East is a festering wound, only without all the charm, and by the time my first book came out, I was tired of picking at it. When I was a twenty-five-year-old law student in New York, I applied for an internship at the Israeli consulate and was surprised to instead be offered a full-time job as a speechwriter for the Israeli Mission to the UN. A bit later, despite not even being Israeli, I was asked to move to Israel to be an English speechwriter for Prime Minister Ariel Sharon. That parade of absurdity was the subject of my book. You should read it, or at very least buy it.

As was apparent to anyone who finished the book, by the time I left Israel after two and a half years of writing speeches, I had had more than enough of the whole situation. I flew back to America, ready to forget the whole thing. But it wasn't as easy to escape as I had hoped.

For starters, I seemed to have unwittingly developed an area of expertise. I don't mean to suggest that I was anything like an actual expert on Israel—my Hebrew was still shaky and I never could figure out why Israelis drank chocolate milk out of a bag instead of a carton—but I'd gained some firsthand knowledge of how the Middle East functioned, or didn't.

As a result, when I decided to get into journalism and started to pitch articles, everyone wanted me to write about the Middle East. So soon I was interviewing former colleagues in the Israeli government and analyzing the always horrible situation for various newspapers and magazines.

The analysis was usually simple:

1. People are killing each other.
2. That is nothing compared to the threat of violence on the horizon.
3. There is a glimmer of hope that things will be worked out for the best.
4. But they probably won't.

It didn't take a Ph.D. in Middle East Studies to put together this incisive analysis. I made frequent phone calls to interview people in Israel, but because I was now back in North America, many of the experts I was contacting were in the United States. I spoke with American politicians and their aides; lobbyists; Middle East activists of various stripes; military folks; and fund-raisers. And as I published more articles, I was approached by more and more laypeople. Laypeople whose convictions were firmer and more entrenched than any I had encountered in the Middle East itself.

"We should attack Iran," an audience member at one of my speaking events would say, leaving it entirely unclear who she meant by "we" or if she herself was willing to join in the fighting.

"I prefer to think of Hezbollah as political activists, not terrorists," someone else would write in an email, which to me sounded like arguing that Italy was not really a country, but more like a pizza party.

It was all a bit overwhelming. Before I'd found myself entangled with the Israeli government, I hadn't known all that much about the Middle East situation. By the time I finished my stint abroad, my eyes had been opened wide to the dysfunctional way the region often worked. But I still had the vague idea that if the situation were being handled by the people I'd grown up with— by those from New York or Los Angeles or Toronto—then everything could have been solved by now.

It turned out that I was horribly wrong. As soon as I started to work as a journalist, I was blown away by the fervency and emotion that discussions of the Middle East elicited in North America. Everyone I encountered—whether they fell on the right among the hawks or on the left among the doves, whether they were Jew, non-Jew, or Arab—seemed sure that if they were just given six months and the authority, they could solve the Middle

East conflict once and for all. Probably without leaving their arm-chairs, or taking a break from yelling at CNN.

Even in Israel, where I'd interacted with Israelis from all over the political spectrum, or at the UN, where I had met various Arab officials, I had encountered very few true Fundamentalists. The majority of those who actually lived in the region dealt with the issue of peace in a practical way, and they seemed to have a firmer grasp of the realities of the situation. For the most part, they seemed to realize that very little could be cast in black-and-white terms, and that the only way to achieve anything in the peace process was to be pragmatic rather than strictly ideological.

Not so in the West, where there was no room for nuance when discussing the Middle East. People I encountered here were set in their opinions. Something as trivial as reality was never going to change their minds.

Shortly after I returned from Israel and started writing about my experiences in the Middle East, I began to get requests to appear as a guest on radio and television shows. The invitations came in from right-wing shows, left-wing shows, shows aimed at Jewish listeners, and even from Al Jazeera. It was at one of the first of these—a show that was broadcast on national television in Canada—that I realized just how nasty and unproductive these discussions could get.

I had received a phone call from a producer asking me if I would be a part of a panel discussion. The panel, along with a studio audience and the audience at home, would watch a documentary about Palestinian prisoners in Israeli jails. After that, we could discuss it and field questions from the audience.

Sure, I thought. *Why not?*

Well, soon I would find out exactly why not.

On the day of the show, I arrived at the studio and met the producer in the lobby, along with Harris, a political activist from Washington, and Oded, the Israeli who had made the film.

"You three are the moderates on the panel," the producer told us, and we looked at one another as if trying to discern signs of ideological affinity.

There were a fair number of people involved, the producer explained, among them far-left activists, far-right, pro-Israel activists, former Palestinian prisoners, and Norman Finkelstein, a controversial professor at DePaul University in Chicago.

I was peripherally aware that, at the time, Finkelstein was in the midst of a battle to get academic tenure. The child of Holocaust survivors, he was a vocal and acerbic critic of Israel, and his tenure application process had turned highly political.

He and Alan Dershowitz, the Harvard Law School professor and ardent supporter of Israel, were engaged in what amounted to verbal warfare. A few years earlier, Finkelstein had published a book devoted to attacking Dershowitz's Middle East stance and accusing him of plagiarism. Dershowitz had reportedly tried to stop the book from being published—apparently asking Governor Arnold Schwarzenegger to intervene, since the book was published by the University of California Press. The two academics were now involved in an ongoing personal conflict. Some were even saying that Dershowitz had tried to dissuade DePaul from granting Finkelstein tenure.

Oded disappeared with one of the producers, and Harris and I were led into one of the green rooms, where assorted people were waiting for the show to start. I couldn't identify some of them, but one group was clearly the former Palestinian prisoners. Looking at them, I thought of my stint in the Israeli government. I had begun it with a reflexive support for Israel and its policies; by the time I had finished, I still only wished the country the best, but had begun to see more complexity in the issues than before.

Still, while I knew that Israel often locked up Palestinians for what might seem to an outsider like mild offenses—throwing stones at heavily armored tanks, for example—I also thought that a solid portion of jailed Palestinians were there for good reason. So I couldn't help but wonder who exactly I was sharing the stage with.

Eventually, we were called to the studio. There, scattered among the bright lights and camera equipment, were about a hundred audience members. Our chairs were labeled with our names and set up in a circle. The audience sat around us in a bigger circle.

One of the Palestinian former prisoners was seated directly beside me, and we greeted each other and shook hands. We made small talk and I wondered what he would think once he found out that I had been a mouthpiece of the government that imprisoned him. I didn't know if he had tried to blow up Israelis or if he had just sworn at the wrong border guard, but I did know that he had recently been in an Israeli jail and I had recently been in the Israeli government, and we were chatting just like two strangers seated beside each other at a wedding—one from the groom's side and the other from the bride's.

Before anyone on the panel was officially introduced, we watched the movie together. It was a portrayal of the culture and difficult conditions Palestinian prisoners had to weather in Israeli jails. I thought it was interesting but fairly innocuous—from what I knew about Israel, it wouldn't have been particularly controversial there, where criticism of the state's policies from a multitude of different angles was the norm.

But, as it turned out, the video was extremely controversial on this side of the world. Right after the movie ended, the host launched the discussion and it quickly grew heated. A few right-leaning panelists denounced the film for being too sympathetic to the Palestinians and not mentioning Israeli suffering. Some on the left criticized it for not showing what they believed to be the true extent of the plight of Palestinian prisoners. For a long while, the Palestinian former prisoners stayed quiet, but when the host asked the one beside me to speak about his impression of the movie, he said that his experiences had been much more grueling than those portrayed in the film. This enraged the far-right activists, who started yelling. That, in turn, enraged the far-left activists, who started yelling louder. Things were not going well.

The host only introduced his guests after they jumped into the fray. And since I'd quickly realized that this was not an argument I wanted any part of, I was not opening my mouth. So I just sat up there—a silent, nameless figure on a violently heated panel.

Soon the argument had veered away from the movie itself and back toward the old hackneyed Middle East debate. Those on the far Left talked about colonization, checkpoints, and brutal Israeli soldiers. The panelists on the far Right talked about terrorism, suicide bombing, and biblical land claims. Those on the Left seemed to believe that Israel was the cause of all of the Middle East's problems, as well as the deficiencies in American foreign policy. To the Right, Israel was always correct—even if its security measures were disproportionate or its settlement policies unproductive. The panelists on the Left thought that any measures Israel took to protect its citizens' lives were discriminatory, that its policies were designed to oppress the Palestinians, and although they didn't say it explicitly, it sounded like their prescription was for Israel just to simply cease to exist. Those on the Right thought that every waking thought of each Palestinian was to kill all the Jews on the planet. When they looked at a Palestinian, all they saw was Hitler. As they argued, in louder and louder voices, it was almost as if the two sides couldn't even hear each other at all.

A few times Harris and a couple of the other relatively restrained people managed to push their way into the conversation, trying to strike some kind of middle ground before being yelled back into silence. It was during one of these exchanges that I noticed an interesting little aside.

In the front row of the audience, just behind my Palestinian neighbor and me, were a couple of his friends. Before the show had started, they had been chatting a bit in English, and had greeted me as well, unaware of my backstory. Now, as Harris and a few other nonfanatics tried—more or less vainly—to have their voices heard, one of these audience members leaned forward to speak to his friend, the Palestinian former prisoner beside me.

"It's easier to deal with the extreme Zionists," he whispered. "Much harder to deal with the moderates."

The Palestinian nodded in agreement. With the panelists screaming tired clichés back and forth, it was the most interesting observation I'd heard so far.

Meanwhile, the shouting continued, and I remained quiet, increasingly aware that I was the only one who wasn't getting involved, while a studio and television audience looked on, probably wondering why I'd been put on the panel in the first place. Self-conscious, I started staring downward to avoid the camera, which meant that I found myself looking directly at Norman Finkelstein's socks.

Wow, I thought, *Norman Finkelstein is wearing some pretty flamboyant socks.*

They were a medley of colors in an intricate pattern, and as I continued to stare at them as a distraction, I wondered if he always wore socks like that or if he had just chosen to wear them because he was on TV. Anyone watching the show would have seen a group of people ferociously debating the Middle East, and one person staring at his copanelist's feet.

Eventually, the host asked for members of the studio audience to comment, and a succession of them did, mostly spouting the same angry arguments aired by the panelists, only in far less lucid forms.

The final one, though, brought the emotional pitch up a notch. He was a teenager of Palestinian descent, but English was his native tongue, and it was clear that he was just as North American as me. Immediately after getting ahold of the microphone, he launched a barrage of angry insults at the right-wing pro-Israel crowd on the panel, berating them and accusing them of "stealing my country."

One of the panelists took the bait and started yelling back.

"But it's not your country!" he screamed. "It's *our* country!"

The teenager's eyes started to tear up, and he continued to scream until his microphone was taken away and everyone was quieted down.

It wasn't really either of their countries, I thought. They both lived on the other side of the world, and enjoyed the kind of security and peace of mind that those living in the region—both Israeli and Palestinian—could only dream of. But they both believed they had the answer to the conflict, just like everyone else on the panel.

And that's when I decided that I would be the one to finally make Middle East peace. If nothing else, I figured, it would shut everyone up.

By the time I began my book tour, the idea had crystallized in my mind.

I would speak to as many people as possible from all over the political spectrum—from the biggest players in the Middle East debate to the cranks who kept bombarding my email in-box—and I would try to figure out what each of them was proposing. In doing so, I hoped to better understand America's perspective on the issue, and maybe even come to some solution. The 2008 presidential campaign was about to begin, and all signs suggested that the Middle East would play a serious role in the results of the election—and that the results of the election would play a serious role in the Middle East.

Over the coming months, I would meet with the various factions and explore the full range of theories—from the sensible to the totally crackpot. I'd participate in some of the outlandish activities that the Middle East debate spawned in North America and try my hand at peacemaking as a sort of freelance diplomat.

Even though I was tired of talking about Israel, I was excited about my journey. I thought that, in a curious way, it might be my only way to escape the conflict. At the very least, hopefully, I would begin to understand why so many people were so obsessed with the subject—and why I myself could not stop engaging with it, despite being absolutely sick of the whole thing.

After I finished my book talk that day, drawing approximately the same amount of applause as the man with dementia, several people from the audience approached me, as they usually did at these events. They would tell me their opinions about the Middle East or ask me strange and irrelevant personal questions, like whether or not I was married. As the line formed, I noticed that my "opening act" had stepped forward, and I didn't know what to expect when he made his way to the front of the line.

"Do you live in Israel?" he asked once he had reached me.

"No," I told him. "I did for a little while, but I came back."

"It's nice to meet you!" he said, and shook my hand.

"Thank you very much." I smiled. I was relieved that this conversation was turning out to be quite sensible.

"Do you live in Israel?" he asked again.

I wasn't sure exactly how to proceed, but other people were now asking me questions, which allowed me to move on without seeming too rude. One woman asked me if it was too dangerous for her grandchildren to visit Israel. No, I told her, and urged her to encourage them to go.

"You know there is no such thing as a Palestinian?" a man asked me, starting to repeat a tired argument I had heard many times before. "They only came to the area after the Jews started arriving. The Jews are the real Palestinians."

I just smiled and nodded, which was generally my strategy when arguments from the far Right or the far Left were foisted on me. All the while, I noted that my opening act was still standing around.

At many of the Israel-related events I spoke at, senior citizens made up a good portion of the audience, but that day the average age was even older than usual. This meant that the event organizer had some additional concerns beyond the usual logistics.

"I better go to the table where they're selling your book," she whispered to me as I continued to speak to the handful of people standing around. "There is one old woman who has to be watched. Otherwise she steals books."

Then she was gone to deal with this potential threat, and my opening act was standing right in front of me again.

"Do you live in Israel?" he asked once more.

"No," I told him again. "I did for a little while, but I came back."

"It's nice to meet you!" he said, and shook my hand.

"Thank you very much," I said and smiled.

"Do you live in Israel?" he asked.

The coming months were not going to be easy.

CHAPTER TWO

Neither Left nor Right,
I'm Just Staying Home Tonight

Shortly after I decided to be the one to make peace in the Middle East, I found myself going to a lunch meeting with someone who worked at a Jewish nonprofit in New York. A mutual friend had thought we would get along and that maybe we would be able to work together on a project of some sort.

Only as I arrived at the restaurant, a small Italian place on the Upper East Side, did it occur to me that I had no idea what this person looked like. I just knew that his name was Wayne, and I had the vague idea that he was in his thirties or early forties. So when I walked in, a little late, and found that the only person standing by the door was well into his sixties, I was a bit surprised.

"Wayne?" I asked tentatively.

"Yes," he said with a big smile, shaking my hand.

Okay, I thought, so Wayne was a bit older than I'd anticipated.

"I'm Gregory," I said. "It's nice to meet you. I'm sorry I'm a bit late."

He looked at his watch, and his brow furrowed.

"I actually thought I was a bit early," he told me.

But before we could discuss this any further, the maître d' appeared and asked us if we wanted a table for two.

We told him that we did, and followed him across the restaurant to an empty table. Then, just as we were about to sit down and I was already wondering if it would be appropriate to order appetizers, my lunch companion suddenly stopped.

"Wait," he said, "did you ask me if my name was *Wayne?*"

"Yes!" I said, alarmed.

"My name is Barry," he told me.

He sounded almost apologetic, and we both paused for a long while, assessing the situation.

"Then why did you say yes?" I asked him eventually.

"I thought you had misspoken."

When Wayne arrived and we sat down at our table, I quickly forgot about the awkwardness with Barry. It was impossible to pay attention to anything other than Wayne, who was so full of manic energy that it seemed possible that he would accidentally knock cutlery or glassware onto my lap at any moment. He was English, which I hadn't known before, and as soon as we sat down together, he started swearing profusely. I liked him immediately.

"You were a bloody speechwriter for the Israeli government?" he asked. "How the fucking hell did that happen?"

As politely as I could, I told him to read my book. I had even brought him a copy, and I handed it to him.

"Fuck!" he said for no apparent reason, staring at the cover.

We ordered our food, and Wayne told me about what his organization did. It had very little to do with the Middle East, but it was interesting stuff. Because I had been immersed in Middle East–related activities for a while, I sometimes forgot that organizations like his existed—American Jewish groups who stayed out of the Middle East fray.

Then he asked me what my next project was.

"I'm going to try to make peace in the Middle East," I told him.

"You're shitting me," he said. "Why the fuck would you try to do that?"

Especially because of his English accent, I thought his constant swearing was somehow funny, but the volume at which he was doing it was starting to make me a bit uncomfortable. A group of Asian tourists were eating lunch, and I noticed that a few of them were casting concerned glances in our direction.

I lowered my voice a little, hoping he would follow suit, and told him about my reasoning. I was sick of hearing about the situation in the Middle East, I said, and if solving it myself was the only way to end it, then that was what I had to do. I explained that my plan was to talk to a wide collection of people engaged with the debate, and see if I could broker a solution—guided by the line I had heard from the Palestinian former prisoner's friend about how it was harder to fight a moderate than a radical. In the end, not only would I hopefully put one of the world's longest-

17

running conflicts to rest, I would also write another book about the experience.

"So you're going to spend months talking to all those Israel nutters?" he asked.

"I think I have to," I told him.

He took a sip of his water, and seemed to be considering what I had told him.

"That's fucking stupid," he said.

I wondered if this was going to be the reaction I got from everyone as I tried to move forward on my project, and I asked him why he thought so.

"You've just fucking told me that you're sick of talking about the Middle East and hanging around with all those bloody nutters," he said. "And now you tell me that you're going to waste your time doing more of that when you actually want to be doing something else. Of course that's fucking stupid."

Suddenly I had an idea.

"Will you be one of my advisors?" I asked him.

"What?"

I explained to him that I had been thinking that it might be useful for me to get a handful of people whom I could run ideas by as I proceeded. Wayne wouldn't serve as a political advisor, exactly, but more as a devil's advocate.

"I'll fucking do it," he said. "I'll check up on you, but I'm not doing it because I think it's a good idea—which I don't—or to help the bloody book you might write. I'm doing it because I'm worried about your fucking mental health. I think this is going to destroy you. That's why I'm doing it. I'm worried about your fucking mental well-being. I'm worried about your fucking marriage."

Okay, I thought, *nice to meet you too.*

I had to admit that Wayne might have had a point about my marriage. When my wife, Abby, and I had just started dating, I was speechwriting for the Israeli government in New York and she had to deal with me having to shape my schedule to take into account events halfway across the world. Later, when I was recruited to write speeches in Jerusalem, I had to persuade her to drop out of school to go with me, even though we'd only been dating for six months. She inexplicably agreed, and when we decided we'd had enough of the whole endeavor and moved back to North America, she was relieved that we were leaving the Middle East behind.

So when I first told her that I was seeking to get myself involved in the situation again, even if it was mostly just from our apartment, she was less than thrilled.

"I thought you were done with all that," she said.

"Just when I thought I was out," I told her, "they pull me back in."

She didn't seem to think that was particularly funny, and so I explained to her, as I had to Wayne, that trying my hand at peacemaking might be the only way I could myself escape the grasp of the Middle East.

"Go play your little games," she said, "but when this is over,

I don't want to hear anything more from you about the Middle East. This is it for you."

That seemed reasonable, and I took it as her consent to proceed. There was no denying that it was pretty condescending, but I chose to ignore that. After all, peace in the Middle East depended on it.

Before I actually delved into freelance diplomacy, I decided to announce my intentions.

And the way to do that, I figured, might as well be Facebook. I had only been a user of the site for about a year—having failed to resist its growing dominance—but I had somehow amassed a large network of contacts, many of whom I didn't know at all. They had approached me as a result of my book, my journalism, or just out of the online ether. And many of them frightened me a bit in their fervent obsession with the Middle East and their frequent determination to convey that through Facebook.

In fact, I had been surprised to find that among Facebook's legions of users, there were a good number of people actively involved with the Middle East debate. From high-profile Washington lobbyists to important Israeli journalists, to activists and operatives of all stripes. It was a bit surreal to find them there, but I had connected on Facebook with many of the people I had first encountered in the real world policy debate.

So, on the day I decided to make my plan public, I logged on to change my status update, the little one-liner at the top of

Facebook pages used to keep all your Facebook contacts abreast of your activities. For months, my status update had been blank. I had, apparently, been doing nothing, or at least nothing worth mentioning. Now, though, I had a bold announcement.

I changed it to: "Gregory Levey is Going to Make Peace in the Middle East in Six Months or Less Without Leaving His Apartment."

The responses and replies began flooding in almost immediately, both from actual friends and from my random contacts.

"I'm going to make pasta," my friend Matt wrote in response.

"Good luck!" a college kid in California I didn't know wrote. "Let me know where I can help."

It was impossible to tell if he was being snarky like Matt or if he was sincere.

"God's speed!" wrote a Somali woman whom I'd met in law school.

"Did you steal Olmert's Facebook status?" asked a left-wing Middle East activist I'd once met.

I even got quick responses from a number of people who had engaged with the Middle East in important ways.

"Fine," wrote a Republican operative who had worked as a high-level liaison to the Orthodox Jewish community, "but genocide is cheating."

Then an actual former Mossad officer whom I was in contact with wrote, "Greg, it's not a peace process, but an industry with a revolving conveyor belt of career-minded journalists, clueless peace activists, lazy diplomats, and ivory tower hacks all trying to say they've made a difference. Cynical enough for ya?"

*   *   *

I actually did think that my home office was as good a place as any to start on the journey to solving the Middle East conflict. I had an almost comically large number of books, magazines, and journals about Israel and the Middle East, some of which I hadn't read at all, and I figured a good beginning to my venture would be to bone up on my knowledge.

I'd amassed all the material before and during my stint in the Israeli government, and in the time since, working as a journalist. There were books on the various Middle East wars, on its diverse population groups, and on the different periods in its history, written from all along the political spectrum. Just below *Elvis in Jerusalem* I found *How to Cure a Fanatic*. *The Case for Israel* was beside *The Case Against Israel*. A book about Jews living in Arab lands was beside several books about Arabs living in Israel. There were books ranging from wild conspiracy theory—one went on and on unconvincingly about Israel's supposed connection to the death of Princess Diana—to those that were eminently sensible but dry and academic.

I had an enormous book called *The Palestinian People*, as well as shelves full of books about the broader region, including relatively large sections on Iraq and Saudi Arabia, and books about relevant issues like diplomacy, statecraft, and espionage. Most of the information I would need in order to come up with a plan, I thought, had to be right here.

I picked up Henry Kissinger's *Diplomacy*, and paged through it to a section about the Middle East. He was discussing the 1956

Suez Crisis, when Israel, the United Kingdom, and France had launched military operations against Egypt, only to be forced out by U.S.–sponsored resolutions at the United Nations. On that episode, Kissinger wrote, "It takes perseverance to find a policy which combines the disadvantages of every course of action, or to construct a coalition that weakens every partner simultaneously. Great Britain, France, and Israel managed just that feat."

I knew the historical context that had precipitated that war and its end, but it still always seemed odd from the perspective of the present day. The French had conspired with the Israelis, and the Americans had stopped them at the United Nations? That didn't sound right at all.

I noted, though, that the core issues in the Middle East hadn't really changed—a depressing thought. There was the issue of Israel's security and the right of the Jewish people to have a country of their own in what they saw as their ancestral homeland. But there was also the issue of the Palestinian people's right to self-determination in what they understood to be their own ancestral homeland. Then there were the micro issues—and sticking points—that never changed all that much either. There was the question of the status of Jerusalem and the West Bank. The question of borders. The question of resources. There was the question of whether the Arab world would recognize Israel. And there was the question about the fate and rights of the Palestinian refugees who had been displaced at Israel's founding.

"Often enough, I am asked to predict when and how peace will come to Israel," I read in the memoirs of David Ben-Gurion, Israel's first prime minister. "I am always obliged to give a disappointing answer by confessing that I have no predictions to make."

But many of the other books did make predictions, as well as prescriptions, discussing the assorted plans for peace that had been put forth over the years. They varied in details and structure, but were similar in essential ways and seemed to blend into each other.

There was the Partition Plan. The Allon Plan. Saunders's peace plan. The Barak Offer. Clinton's compromise. The Arab Peace Initiative. The Quartet Road Map. The Geneva Accord. The Oslo Accords. The Disengagement Plan. And that was just a start.

Looking at the list was depressing and dispiriting. None of them had really worked. Would the Levey Plan be able to do any better?

Browsing through my bookshelves, I also discovered some interesting curiosities. A few years ago, for example, a twelve-year-old Arab citizen of Israel had entered a trivia contest about Zionist history—and won. Somehow the kid's knowledge of Israeli history and culture had beaten out his Jewish opponents. I learned that when Ariel Sharon had been commanding forces in the Six-Day War, he had sometimes, in the lulls between battles, lain down on the desert sand and gone quickly and soundly to sleep, to the astonishment of the frazzled soldiers under his command. And that at one point Yasser Arafat had secretly owned a percentage of Bowlmor Lanes, the fancy bowling alley near NYU that I had sometimes bowled at when I was a student there.

I also read about Orde Wingate, a legendary British army officer who had served as a mentor and trainer for some of the early Zionists fighting to establish a state, including Moshe Dayan, later the famous eye-patch-wearing Israeli war hero. Wingate, I read, had lounged in his tent each night, holding forth on military strategy and philosophy to his young Jewish disciples, while using some kind of special, small comb—to brush out his pubic hair.

On that note, I thought, it was time to get started on my plan.

The next step was to try a unique piece of software called Peace-Maker. Invented by Asi Burak, a former captain in Israeli military intelligence, it was designed to simulate the Middle East conflict and educate people on the difficulties and nuances involved in Middle East diplomacy. That sounded like a noble goal to me, since people always had black-and-white views of what was a very complex situation. PeaceMaker had been out for a couple of years, and I had been meaning to give it a shot. Now, at the outset of my quest, it seemed like a good time to do it.

I logged on to the site which, among other things, had a supportive quote from Arun Gandhi, grandson of the Mahatma, and a virtual store selling "PeaceWare." The store carried hats, mugs, and tote bags all sporting the slogan "I wanna be a PeaceMaker." It also carried boxer shorts with PEACEMAKER written on the front. I obviously had to have those, and I quickly ordered them.

Before actually trying the program out, though, I decided to give its creator a call.

"Basically," I told him when I got him on the line, "I'm trying to make peace in the Middle East, and I thought that trying your simulator might be a good way to start."

"Uh-huh," he said.

"I'll be writing a book about the whole thing," I babbled on, "if it all works out."

"I see. But it will be a novel, right? It's fiction?"

"No," I told him, getting a bit tired of having different versions of this same conversation with everyone. "It's nonfiction. I'm actually trying to solve the conflict."

I wanted to ask him how long it would take for my Peace-Maker boxer shorts to arrive, but managed to hold back and ask instead about the process he and his colleagues had used to create PeaceMaker. They had initially designed the game at Carnegie Mellon University's Entertainment Technology Center, using focus groups of Israeli and Palestinian students and then experts from Palestinian and Israeli think tanks and universities to make the simulation react to a decision maker's actions in the same way the Middle East would. These consultants also advised them on small details the designers didn't know about, such as the color of keffiyeh worn by particular factions, in order to make the simulation that much more realistic.

They were very careful about bias in the game, Burak told me, and endeavored to make it symmetrical in difficulty, no matter which side you played. They also wanted to make it "nonlinear," he said, so that your actions in one context didn't lead to the same results if performed in a different political context. For example, if tensions were high within the game and a player tried to implement a confidence-building measure, the result would be very different than if he or she did the same thing when tensions within the game were low.

"Most people don't understand cause and effect in the Middle East," he said. "But they play the game with all the factors in action, and they say to me, 'Now I understand cause and effect.' And they get more sympathetic with the leaders and say, 'Oh, it's tough to be a leader!'"

I asked Burak what was the most interesting thing he learned from people's reactions to the game, and he immediately said it was watching people play the opposite side.

"For example," he said, "I'd see Arabs playing the game from the Israeli side and they'd get frustrated by the actions of Hamas and start bombing them in retaliation. Then they'd try to rationalize it to me, but it was clear they suddenly understood the challenges of the other side better. It's a very profound thing to watch."

When I started the simulator myself, I half expected it to be like playing a video game, which I hadn't really done in about fifteen years. But if I was expecting Super Mario Brothers set in Jerusalem, it only took a moment for me to be disabused of the notion. Somber music started playing, and I started seeing images from the last century of Middle Eastern history. Riots, bombings, tanks, and desperate-looking refugees. Not exactly the light video-game fare I remembered from my childhood.

Then I saw the famous footage from 1993 of Israeli prime

minister Yitzhak Rabin and Yasser Arafat shaking hands on the White House lawn, awkwardly forced together by President Clinton. I had been fifteen years old when that had happened and not politically engaged at all, but even in my oblivious teenage state, I had been able to realize that something momentous and hopeful was happening. Finally the endless conflict that always provided the background noise to other world events would be solved.

Then, of course, everything fell apart. There was another intifada, and more wars, and thousands of deaths—and somewhere in the middle of all that I had briefly worked for the Israeli government—and now here we were again, with Palestinians and Israelis dying, extremists on both sides running amok, and everything even worse than before that fateful handshake.

So far, this video game was just depressing me.

PeaceMaker gave me the choice of playing the Israeli prime minister or the Palestinian president. Since it was the side I understood better, I decided to take the Israeli position for my first try. I then took a few minutes to learn about the various actions I could take as the country's leader. I could use security measures, like covert operations or full-scale military maneuvers. I could engage in political measures, like speaking to the Palestinian leader, the United Nations, or the United States. Or I could build infrastructure for either Israelis or Palestinians.

At the bottom of the screen, there was a panel where I could gauge my approval ratings from the Israeli and Palestinian populations and assess other measures of my progress.

Okay, I thought, starting the simulation up. *Let's make peace.*

And immediately there was a giant suicide bombing in Jerusalem, killing many Israeli civilians. Things weren't off to a good start.

I decided to respond, but in a moderate way, so as to keep the Israeli population satisfied but not inflame the Palestinians too much. Instead of a full-scale military action, I launched a covert operation against a terrorist leader in Gaza. Then I poured money into the Palestinian infrastructure. If their day-to-day lives were improved, I reasoned, they would be less likely to use violence.

But the Palestinian president called my goodwill "condescending," which I couldn't help thinking was rather ungrateful.

My own defense minister was then quoted saying something deeply offensive to the Palestinians, which stirred the tensions even more. *Who is this guy?* I wondered, but the truth was that I remembered events precisely like that derailing Israeli leaders when I worked for the country. The game, so far, was pretty spot-on.

Because I was perceived as being soft on the Palestinian militants, my approval rating among the Israeli population was dropping. To assure them that their security was of paramount importance to me, I continued construction of the controversial security barrier that separated Israel from the Palestinian territories. In real life, I had always thought the barrier was a good idea in principle—these two peoples clearly could not get along, so why not separate them—but I'd never been happy with its route, which went through occupied Palestinian land.

But in PeaceMaker, I had the option of continuing the construction while sticking to the 1949 armistice lines instead of encroaching into the West Bank. I thought it was ideal.

Unfortunately, though, nobody else seemed to agree, and tensions just got worse. There were riots in Gaza and the West Bank, and the Israelis didn't think I was doing enough to protect them.

Grasping at straws, I sent a joint Jewish-Arab orchestra to Europe to demonstrate cultural cooperation. Almost immediately they came back of their own volition, saying that given the current circumstances, it was inappropriate.

Can you guys really make that decision yourselves? I wondered. *I'm the prime minister!*

But the fate of my cultural mission was soon the least of my concerns, as pretty much everyone wanted me out of office, and tensions boiled over completely.

It had only been three weeks of simulation time when the news came. I had caused "the Third Intifada."

Game over.

"It didn't work," I told Abby. "I caused the Third Intifada. And it took only three weeks."

"Let me try," she said, and I shrugged and got up from my desk so that she could sit down at the computer. I watched as she started, but I quickly got bored and left the room. My working assumption, in any case, was that the game was rigged so that it was impossible to actually make peace. I figured that might be the lesson it was teaching.

In fact, I knew that Danny Yatom, a former director of the Mossad and senior Israeli negotiator, had once been asked by the Israeli media to play PeaceMaker—and hadn't had good results either. I had watched the footage online and saw that after just a few minutes of playing, he too had been declared a failure. Yatom had thrown up his hands and declared that nothing could be learned from PeaceMaker.

When I'd asked Asi Burak about that, he laughed a bit and told me that he had to be careful what he said. When Yatom had played, Burak said, he had launched round after round of hard-line military actions against the Palestinians, and only then tried to conduct diplomacy. Even then, however, he hadn't engaged in actual dialogue, but had made demands of the Palestinians. Yatom had claimed that PeaceMaker was unrealistic when these decisions hadn't produced results, saying they were the actions that would be taken in the real world.

At this point, Burak laughed again.

"Yes!" he said. "But they haven't worked in real life either, have they?"

So, while Abby launched into what I assumed would be another fruitless attempt at Middle East peacemaking, I went to our living room to read a bit from the big book I'd found on my shelf called *The Palestinian People*.

"In the middle decades of the twentieth century," I read, "Palestinians developed a self-identity as a people set apart."

Then after a little while, Abby yelled from the office, "I reached the first milestone!"

The first milestone? I had no idea what that was, since I had reached nowhere near that point. I had only caused death and destruction. The first milestone, apparently, had something to do with cooperation with the Palestinian National Authority and some level of autonomy for Gaza. That definitely sounded like progress, but I was sure her success wouldn't last and went back to my book.

"I reached the second milestone!" Abby said a few minutes later.

She had now successfully run Israel's diplomacy for six months of game time, and apparently regional tensions were much lower than when she had started.

Well, good for her, I thought. *But this is all going to end badly anyway.*

But at regular intervals for the next hour or so, she would update me with disturbingly positive news. The Palestinian president was eager to cooperate with her—he had shunned me completely and refused to help me bolster Israel's security against Palestinian terrorist groups—and this was yielding results.

I wasn't following exactly what she was doing, but I probably should have been, since her approval ratings from both the Israeli and Palestinian population continued to climb. Rallies were even being held to show support for her. She soon informed me that a rail link had now been built to connect the Gaza Strip and the West Bank. That sounded utopian—and farfetched. I put my book down and went back into the office to investigate whether she was making it all up.

But just as I got in there, peace was being declared and she was being awarded a peace prize.

"See, it's not that hard," she said.

I smiled, more than a little bitter.

She had taken a fairly dovish strategy, not making any moves that would inflame the situation in the Middle East by angering the Palestinians, but at the same trying to keep the Israeli population assured that she had their security in mind at all times. It was a tightrope wire that she had somehow managed to walk—and apparently the simulator was programmed to reward this approach.

It was now playing triumphant music and showing images of peace and cooperation. But even though Abby had beaten the game on her first attempt—not to mention making peace in the Middle East—I noticed that she looked a little upset.

"What's wrong?" I asked, confused.

"It's sad," she said. "It feels so good, but you just can't help but wish it were real."

CHAPTER THREE

The Israel Lobby
and the Perfect Avocado

I waited anxiously for my PeaceMaker boxer shorts to arrive. Meanwhile, though, I knew I had to move on without them. After my disastrous attempt at making virtual peace, I was considering my next move carefully. I had decided that it might be time to venture out of the apartment—even for a little while—to ask for advice. And I knew who I wanted to ask.

Just down the street was a fruit stand run by a Palestinian grocer. Or at least I thought he was Palestinian. Dealing with Middle East issues for the past few years, I had interacted with a good numbers of Arabs and was sometimes able to identify which area of the Arab world they came from. I thought this grocer looked either Palestinian or Jordanian, or possibly Lebanese. In any case, I figured he might have some valuable insights that all the supposed experts didn't.

I knew, though, that if I wanted to break the ice and start

talking politics with him, it would have to be a gradual process. I couldn't just walk in there and say, "Can I please have some carrots? Oh, and, what did you think of the progress made at the recent summit of the Middle East Quartet?"

I needed to move slowly and gain his trust before he would open up to me. To do this I would have to become a regular customer. But this presented a problem.

"Their produce is terrible," Abby said when I told her my plan.

"I know, I know," I said.

It really was. I normally would have wanted to support a little independent business rather than the big supermarket farther down the street, but I generally avoided it, because every time I had bought produce there, it had been absolutely awful.

"We can't start buying from him," Abby said. "His stuff is disgusting."

But in the interests of Middle East peace, I thought, we would have to make sacrifices. Mealy peaches or overripe blackberries might need to be among them. So the next morning I headed straight to the stand, smiled at the grocer, and struggled to find a perfect avocado. After a while, I found a few that seemed, at best, edible.

"Hi," I said, hoping for some conversation, but all he did was nod and ring up my purchase.

When I tried the avocados at home, they tasted like soap.

But I persisted. Whenever I was walking by, I'd stop in and buy some moldy apples or some potatoes that tasted like sour milk, and I would awkwardly try to make small talk. After a while, he began to recognize me, but this was admittedly a long way from discussing international law or the contours of a potential peace.

Meanwhile, our apartment was overflowing with mediocre fruit and vegetables.

"Why did you get so much asparagus?" Abby would ask.

"I had to," I'd say. "I was hanging out with the grocer again."

Sure, it was asparagus now, I thought, but it was only a matter of time before the grocer and I were engaging with the core ideas of the Middle East problem.

Those ideas weren't hard to come by from other directions. The last few years had seen turbulence and upheaval, not just in the Middle East—which was par for the course—but also in the war of ideas *about* the region that was constantly waged in the West. There were new lobbying organizations forming, fresh voices on the issues, and some important new currents in the debate.

One of these new developments had first broken when I was living in Israel, and I still remembered that morning well. I'd noticed that an article had come out in the *London Review of Books* called "The Israel Lobby." Written by John Mearsheimer and Stephen Walt, two respected political scientists—Mearsheimer was at the University of Chicago and Walt was at Harvard—it was clearly going to cause controversy.

"The Israel Lobby" argued that, for decades, the heart of U.S. Middle East policymaking had revolved around Israel and that this had directly resulted in animosity being targeted at the United States from the Arab and Muslim world. More cuttingly, it suggested the relationship between the U.S. and Israel did not result from some deep overlap of strategic assets, but from a powerful domestic lobby in the United States that drove American policy along a trajectory divorced from real U.S. national interests, a lobby that also stifled opposing voices. It supposedly consisted of lobbyists, journalists, government officials, and fund-raisers—many of them Jewish.

Rather than "shared strategic interests or compelling moral imperatives," Walt and Mearsheimer wrote in their essay, "the thrust of US policy in the region derives almost entirely from domestic politics, and especially the activities of the 'Israel Lobby.' Other special-interest groups have managed to skew foreign policy, but no lobby has managed to divert it as far from what the national interest would suggest, while simultaneously convincing Americans that US interests and those of the other country—in this case, Israel—are essentially identical."

Coming as this did from highly reputable academics, it was sure to be a bombshell.

But when the article came out, and I asked a top official in the Israeli government if he had seen the piece, he didn't seem fazed by it at all. For him, it was just the latest incarnation of an old anti-Semitic forgery, and so it could be dismissed without being addressed at all; when I offered to give him a copy, he didn't even want to look at it.

"Eh," he said, waving his hand to dismiss it. "It's just *The Protocols of the Elders of Zion* again."

The Protocols, of course, was the famous forgery from czarist Russia that depicted a Jewish plot to control the world's levers of power. In the West, they had long been regarded as nonsense. But in the Arab world, they were seen as legitimate even today.

In fact, friends who had visited the various Arab capitals had told me that Arabic copies of them were prominently displayed in bookstores and souvenir shops in those cities.

I thought the Israeli official's dismissive attitude was a misguided, and perhaps even dangerous, one. The little synopsis I read online definitely made the article seem replete with exaggerations, but I thought that ignoring a major article by respected researchers in an important publication was probably not a good strategy for Israel to take. If there were any grains of truth in the piece at all, it would probably get some traction.

Over the next few weeks, Israel's most vocal defenders in the United States came out swinging, some of them leveling accusations of anti-Semitism and others attacking the article and its authors on more substantive grounds. In a *Washington Post* op-ed titled "Yes, It's Anti-Semitic," Eliot A. Cohen, another prominent political scientist, called it a "wretched piece of scholarship." He also pointed out that white supremacist David Duke had endorsed Walt and Mearsheimer's article.

Alan Dershowitz, meanwhile, posted a forty-five-page response on Harvard University's website, in which he wrote:

This study is so filled with distortions, so empty of originality or new evidence, so tendentious in its tone, so lacking in nuance and balance, so unscholarly in its approach, so riddled with obvious factual errors that could easily have been checked (but obviously were not), and so dependent on biased, extremist and anti-American sources, as to raise the question of motive: what would motivate two well-recognized academics to depart so grossly from their usual standards of academic writing and research in order to produce a "study paper" that contributes so little to the existing scholarship while being so susceptible to misuse?

The morning that I first saw Walt and Mearsheimer's essay was many months ago now, but the controversy stirred up by it continued to rage. They followed their article with the publication of a book-length version, accompanied by a barrage of publicity—and a simultaneous flurry of debate.

In fact, Abe Foxman, national director of the Anti-Defamation League, published his own book at the same time called *The Deadliest Lies: The Israel Lobby and the Myth of Jewish Control*. In it, he provided an array of counterarguments to Walt and Mearsheimer's claims and suggested that the allegations they were making were really driven by an anti-Semitic narrative.

Even in just scanning the original article to get a sense of it, I had seen that it had logical problems. For instance, the very loose constellation of characters and organizations that Walt and Mearsheimer grouped together was too divergent to be reasonably considered a unified lobby. It included so many individuals and groups across the American political and journalistic landscape as to be just about incoherent.

But some of their argument was provocative. There was no question that there were powerful interests in the American political landscape that drove policy in ways that weren't necessarily indicative of how the majority of Americans would feel if they actually considered the issues. And, I thought, in ways that sometimes weren't even in the American interest, in the sense that they often deepened the level of anger in the Arab world toward the United States. As a low-level employee of the Israeli government, even I had dealt with some lobbyists and operatives from the United States and elsewhere whose actions seemed a little skewed—more aggressively pro-Israel than the Israeli government itself.

Even so, there were many aspects of their argument that made me quite uncomfortable, because at times the two political scientists seemed to come very close to pointing the finger at American Jews as a dangerous fifth column. I knew some people would read it and reflexively label it anti-Semitic, and although I definitely did not want to be like that—muzzling debate and minimizing real anti-Semitism—I too felt there was something unseemly about an article that could be construed as an argument that The Jews were controlling the government.

Although I wrote a bit about the controversy for some magazines, I mostly ignored the debate. Then something odd happened. I heard that several of *my own* journalistic articles about how DC lobbyists affected U.S.–Middle East policymaking were cited in the book-length version of the article titled "The Israel Lobby and U.S. Foreign Policy." This took me aback a bit, and pushed me to think about the argument more.

On the one hand, I definitely found some of what the authors were discussing compelling and important. Middle East policy did often seem highly influenced by various interest groups, which included not just pro-Israel sorts, but also those connected to the oil establishment, who could never be said to be pro-Israel at all. The heart of the matter was that these forces and others—such as the weapons supply industry and pressure groups formed by Evangelical Christians—held significant sway over U.S. policy in the Middle East. On the other hand, it seemed reductive to ascribe so much power to the so-called Israel Lobby, and a bit simplistic. But after finding out that some of my own work was actually referred to in the book, I felt I should at least read it and see what had been changed or added to the original article.

Some of the academic sloppiness the article's critics had pointed at had been addressed, but the essence of it remained the same. Walt and Mearsheimer argued that American support for Israeli policy was often misplaced and was driven less by American national interests than by the influence of those grouped into their "Lobby"—Jewish organizations, lobbyists, journalists, and policymakers. Further, according to Walt and Mearsheimer, it was extremely difficult for anyone to actually discuss this situation openly.

"The real reason why American politicians are so deferential," they wrote, "is the political power of the Israel lobby."

The authors were criticized—and occasionally praised—in almost every publication I could think of, and appeared on a multitude of television and radio programs as well. If debate on the Israel issue was being stifled, it certainly wasn't evident from their situations.

For my own project, I decided that approaching them might be interesting, and when I did, Stephen Walt gave me a day and time to call him in his office at Harvard.

* * *

Meanwhile, it was my friend Luke's birthday, and we arranged to meet at the pub down the street to have a celebratory beer. I ended up getting to the corner a little early and, to kill time, I crossed the road to the fruit stand. Normally I came in during the day, but this was a little before ten at night. Maybe, I thought, there would be a different vibe.

I walked in and quickly picked out some fruit and vegetables. A cucumber, some blackberries, a bag of carrots, and an apple. I didn't even examine the produce at all, and was essentially just grabbing things off the shelf randomly. As I did this, the grocer watched me warily. When I brought the produce up to the counter and he started ringing it all up, I decided to raise my level of intensity.

"How are you?" I asked. "How's the night going?"

A little desperate as I asked this, I even found myself using the cheesiest of all hand gestures: the rolling, double finger gun.

"I'm okay," he said, stepping back a bit. "Thank you."

He seemed frightened, I thought. This whole grocer thing was really not going as planned at all. I paid him for the groceries, but wasn't quite ready to give up yet.

"You have a good rest of the night now, okay?" I said, hating myself a little for how I was acting.

"I will." He nodded, clearly wanting me to leave. I half-wanted to bring up my upcoming conversation with Stephen Walt and ask him his opinion on it, but that seemed a bit premature.

And as I walked back out into the street, it occurred to me that part of the problem was that the grocer almost certainly thought I was hitting on him. After all, I kept showing up and making awkward small talk, while lingering a bit too long, making strange hand gestures, and buying inordinate amounts of produce.

When I arrived at the pub, Luke was there, and I handed him the bag.

"Here," I said, a bit dejected. "Happy birthday."

"Why are you giving me a bag of produce?" he asked, looking inside, and I proceeded to tell him what was going on. He just shook his head and put the bag down on the table.

"So this isn't working at all yet," he said, and I had to agree.

"And there's also another problem," I told him. "To be honest, I'm beginning to suspect that the grocer might actually be Mexican."

Unfortunately, this was the truth. As the days wore on and we hadn't had a real conversation, let alone one about the peace process, I was even starting to doubt my ability to recognize the grocer's descent.

"If he does turn out to be Mexican," I told Luke, shrugging, "at least I'll be able to get the Mexican perspective on the Middle East conflict."

"How is the rest of it going?" Luke asked, ignoring what I had just said. I told him about my failed attempt at PeaceMaker, and about the Israel Lobby and the conversation I was going to have with Stephen Walt.

"I'm just at a fact-finding stage," I rationalized. "I'm trying to learn before actually going forward with making peace."

What I didn't tell him was that I was starting to feel the first little flickers of doubt about my project. In the end, I wondered, was I just playing video games, making awkward phone calls to strangers, and harassing my local grocer?

What am I doing? I worried intermittently. *Where is all this leading me?*

But I didn't admit any of that to Luke. I just made more allusions to "fact finding," while staring hard at the bag of subpar produce I had given my friend as a birthday gift, and nodding in a way that I imagined looked shrewd.

I called Stephen Walt a couple of days later. Before we launched into our discussion, he asked the same question as everyone else. What exactly was I doing?

"I'm trying to personally solve the Middle East conflict," I said, for what already seemed like the hundredth time.

At this, he paused, but then had a slightly different response than the others I had been getting.

"That's sort of what I was trying to do as well," he said. "Good luck to you."

I laughed a little uncomfortably, not entirely sure how to understand that statement. Then I asked him what he thought of the current direction of the Middle East.

"The trends are very discouraging if you play out the current set of policies," he said. "Even beside theories of demographic shift, with generational changes and the reverse aliyah problem, it's not clear where the happy ending is. I'm by nature optimistic, but given the hardened attitudes on both sides, at the moment it's hard to see a good result."

There was a lot in this statement to unpack, but I chose to focus on what he called the "reverse aliyah problem," and asked him to explain what he meant by it.

Aliyah, which is a Hebrew word that literally means "ascendancy," is used to describe a Jewish person's immigration to Israel. Since even before the creation of the Jewish state, Zionists have called out for Jews from across the world to "make aliyah" in order to complete the "Ingathering of the Exiles" that Israel's creation was intended to represent. A number of organs of the Israeli government are tasked with facilitating aliyah, and they are aided by several outside organizations. There is even a long list of trips and special programs for Jewish youths and families living in the Diaspora that are explicitly intended to entice them into making aliyah. They're sponsored by Jewish organizations, Jewish and Christian philanthropists, and the Israeli government, and although they differ tremendously in focus—from religious-based tours to trips that focus on the social and nightlife opportunities for young people in the Holy Land—for many of these programs, pushing immigration to Israel is the goal. Aliyah was the engine that drove Israel's first half century of existence. It was initially its reason for existing, and it then became the source of much of its energy and potential.

So what did Walt mean by the "reverse aliyah problem"?

Reverse aliyah, for Walt, was just what it sounded like. Frustrated by the dangers and difficulties of living in Israel, or tempted by the opportunities offered elsewhere, a lot of Israelis were leaving the country. Further, many Jews from elsewhere who had immigrated to Israel were finding themselves in over their heads and departing. In addition, even many of the Israelis who were not abandoning the country completely were half-abandoning it, or preparing to abandon it. They were splitting their time between homes in Israel and homes abroad, sending their children to foreign universities, or just clamoring to get second passports—suggesting, Walt argued, that they were seeking "escape hatches." To some extent this had always been an issue for Israel, but he believed it was increasing at a fairly rapid clip and would become a real problem before too long.

Why, though, was this a problem for those hoping for Middle East peace? Sure, it presented a drain of human capital for Israel, but what were the implications for the peace process?

According to Walt, the majority of those Israelis leaving the country or securing escape hatches were, as one would expect, the more cosmopolitan ones—and those more at ease with the outside world. Usually, he said, this meant that they were more broad-minded and the people perhaps more amenable to compromise. In the long run, the fact that *they* were leaving, or preparing to leave, might mean that Israel's willingness to make concessions for peace might dissipate. Combined with a hardening of attitudes among the Palestinians, that was a potentially lethal combination.

"It's possible to imagine a world," Walt told me, "where both populations get even more uncompromising."

And that is what he proposed was happening.

I changed tacks a bit, and asked Walt if he was happy that he and his cowriter had published *The Israel Lobby* and with how things had gone since then.

"I'm very glad we wrote it," he said. "That's what academics are supposed to do—tackle big and important questions."

He paused for a moment, and when he spoke again, it sounded to me like he was choosing his words carefully.

"Given the environment," he went on, "I'm reasonably pleased with how things have gone. Our major goal was to get a discussion started on something that had become taboo in mainstream foreign policy circles. Veiled comments or hushed conversations were allowed, but not open discussion. I thought that was an unhealthy situation."

"Do you think your book had an effect?" I asked.

"Because of a combination of individual activity and conditions in the world, I think there has been an effect," he said. "There was our book and Jimmy Carter's book."

Jimmy Carter had published a book around the same time called *Palestine: Peace Not Apartheid,* which directed heated criticism against Israeli settlements in the Palestinian territories and their effect on the peace process.

"Carter didn't retreat or shrink back," Walt said. "He got out there and gave lots of talks. People can disagree with his views, but Carter has a well-deserved reputation of being a very moral, principled person. That gave him a lot of credibility."

It was interesting, I thought, how one's opinion about Carter could serve as a sort of litmus test. Many of the people I knew in the pro-Israel establishment had a firmly entrenched distaste— even hatred—for Jimmy Carter. And credibility was the absolute last thing they would have ascribed to the former president.

"Carter," I'd once heard one say with a dismissive snort. "He just wants to finish what Hitler started."

According to Walt, Carter's book as well as his own, in addition to the growing prominence of the blogosphere and some new developments in the political landscape, were helping to create changes in the dynamics of the debate. Although I definitely didn't agree with his reductive analysis of the U.S.-Israel relationship, I had to agree with him that these factors had opened up the Middle East discussion over the past couple of years.

"There's a little bit more oxygen now," he told me, "but it's still difficult to publish things like this in the United States, and you pay something of a price."

It was now time, I thought, to pose a more direct question.

"How should I go about solving the Middle East conflict?" I asked him.

"The most important step that could be made now is to have an open and honest discourse about the history of the region," he said. "The more you understand what has happened, the more you'll be able to see what has to be done."

When I put down the phone, I spent a while considering the call. Walt had seemed fairly reasonable. It was hard to see him as the raving anti-Semite some had made him out to be. I reminded myself, though, that it had been said many times before that genteel anti-Semitism was the most dangerous kind. Nobody was going to buy a skinhead pundit or a neo-Nazi scholar, but a smooth-talking person who *seemed* well intentioned might all too easily slip by.

Still, it just hadn't really sounded like that's what he was when I talked to him. My impression was that he was being sincere and honestly believed that the accusations against him were unfounded and that his work was making a positive contribution to peacemaking efforts by widening the parameters of debate in a constructive way. This didn't mean it actually was, of course, because there was still the possibility that he could be wildly deluded.

Were he and his compatriots really trying to contribute to Middle East peace as he told me, I wondered, or were their intentions as malicious as others claimed?

I decided to email Wayne, the foul-mouthed Brit, to ask him his thoughts on Stephen Walt and the Israel Lobby. He had agreed to be my advisor, after all. So I wrote to him and told him that I needed his advice.

I sat back and waited for a response, but none came. Instead, a few minutes later, I received an email invitation to attend a conference in Washington.

The invitation came from an official who worked for AIPAC, the American Israel Public Affairs Committee. If there was one organization that most exemplified what Walt and Mearsheimer called the "Israel Lobby," it was AIPAC, the influential and sometimes controversial pro-Israel lobby group based in Washington DC. The *New York Times* has described it as "the most important organization affecting Israel's relationship with Israel," and indeed, it always came up in any discussion of the American–Israeli relationship.

AIPAC was founded as an advocacy boutique in the 1950s, but as its own website attested, it had "grown into a 100,000 member national grassroots movement," led by a professional staff in Washington. It was involved in advocacy and lobbying of both Congress and, to a lesser degree, the White House, to help steer American policy in what it considered a pro-Israel direction. A bipartisan organization, it had close relationships with members of Congress from both parties—and backed those politicians and candidates whose views on Israel it supported. Its membership was mostly Jewish but also included other dedicated supporters of Israel, and its mission was to protect Israel's security—often by pushing an unflinchingly hard line on the Jewish state's right to defend itself.

AIPAC was attacked in certain quarters. In some people's minds it was the embodiment of the nefariousness that Walt and Mearsheimer wrote about, the puppet master pulling the strings of American policy. Or, even more ominously, it was alluded to by some in quintessentially anti-Semitic terms, fitting age-old racist narratives: the Jews controlling the government. In fact, over the years there had even been the occasional call for AIPAC to register as a foreign agent, which would have both stigmatized and hamstrung the organization.

But the criticism didn't only come from the American side of the Atlantic. Left-wing pundits in Israel often critiqued it as well, and when I had served in the Israeli government, I had sometimes even heard some of the more dovish Israeli officials express frustration at the hawkishness of AIPAC. For example, when there were tentative Israeli moves toward rapprochement with Syria, the resistance of many in the AIPAC fold to encourage similar American moves was a thorn in the Israeli side. And when Yitzhak Rabin was prime minister of Israel in the 1990s, he crossed swords with AIPAC a number of times, publicly accusing it of interfering in matters best left to the government of Israel.

Meanwhile, many political analysts on the Right, the Center, and even the Left had much more benign assessments of the organization. Lobbying, after all, is an important and entirely constitutional part of the way that the American system of government works. There are lots of different lobbies representing various interests, some of them—like the NRA—more powerful than AIPAC, and some of them pushing particular viewpoints on foreign affairs. Moreover, AIPAC was just doing what it could to ensure that an important American ally and strategic asset in the Middle East received the support needed to maintain its security. It was just reminding American government where its priorities should rightfully be.

As usual, I felt that there was probably some middle ground between the conflicting views. I had certainly sometimes seen AIPAC step rightward of the views I thought were held by most Americans and even by many Israelis—and push American policy in that direction. At the same time, I didn't think there was anything too conspiratorial going on and that the people of AIPAC were well intentioned, really doing what they believed was in the best interests of both Israel and the United States.

But one thing I was positive about was something that everyone seemed to agree on: AIPAC was important. I was at least going to have to come to understand it better, which was why the invitation from one of its officials was tempting. I knew him from some journalistic work I had done, and he had always been welcoming and open.

"Come down to Washington," he said. "Come to our policy conference."

The AIPAC "policy conference" was a sort of yearly Woodstock for AIPAC's membership, both for its grassroots activists and for its high-level operatives and their allied politicians. The problem was that attending would mean having to venture farther from my apartment than just the grocer on the street corner.

At one point in the next few days, as I weighed whether to go down to DC for the policy conference, I wandered into the little grocery kiosk. Halfheartedly picking up a pineapple and heading up to the grocer at his cash register, I noticed something was a bit different in the store. Instead of the radio, the kiosk's little speaker system was playing Arabic music.

Hearing it, I paused on my way up to the register, still holding the pineapple. Yes, it was definitely Arabic music.

Good, I thought, *at least I'm not totally off base in my ethnic profiling. Unless, of course, he is a Mexican who just happens to like Arabic music.*

Approaching the counter, I started bobbing my head to the music, as if this were my favorite song. And then something amazing happened: the grocer saw me doing that, and he started bobbing his head too. Then we bobbed our heads together.

Years before, I had briefly studied Arabic, but almost nothing had stuck. I was able to say "I'm studying Arabic at New York University," but that wasn't very useful in conversation, and hadn't actually been true for years. I couldn't say or understand much else.

As a result, as the grocer and I bobbed our heads in unison, it occurred to me that I had no idea what the lyrics I was acting so enthusiastic about might mean.

"The Jewish infidel monkey dogs must be driven into the sea," the singer might have been saying. Or possibly it was just the Arabic version of "Don't tell my heart, my achy breaky heart."

I was sure, though, that he was not singing about how he was studying Arabic at New York University. I would have been able to catch that.

In any case, I continued bobbing my head and smiling, and so did the grocer, until it started to feel a little weird.

This was only going to make it seem even more like I was hitting on him, I thought. And when it felt like this had been going on forever—the two of us bobbing our heads together to the Arabic music while I held a pineapple—I knew I had to end it.

"What language is that?" I asked, even though I knew. I thought this might be a bridge to conversation.

He told me it was Arabic, and then I asked him where he was from, and he told me he was from Lebanon—but of Palestinian descent. Finally I was getting some traction, I thought, and it was a lot easier than eating bad produce for months on end.

But just as I was about to try to take the next step and casually bring up Middle East politics—"So, how 'bout them Hezbollah? How do you like their chances this season?"—another customer arrived at the cash register with some items to purchase.

"Don't do it," I wanted to tell her. "The produce here is terrible. I'm just here for the geopolitical consulting."

But I let her go in front of me, and the moment passed. I'd have to continue this conversation when I came back from AIPAC.

CHAPTER FOUR

What Happened in Romania

I was at my desk, planning my trip down to Washington for AIPAC, when my phone rang. I answered it, and the woman on the other end of the line told me that she was a television news producer.

"We wanted to know if you'd come on the show in a few hours to talk about what happened today at the meeting about the Middle East," she said.

I paused. I had no idea what meeting she was even talking about, and since I followed the situation in the region pretty closely, that was odd.

"Sure," I said after a moment's reflection. "I'd be happy to talk about what happened at the meeting."

I probably wouldn't normally have agreed to appear on TV to talk about something I knew nothing about, but I thought this might be useful for my own project. And anyway, I reasoned, I'd just look up what happened at whatever meeting they were talking about and hopefully I'd be more or less okay to speak about it on TV.

So a few hours later I was on my way to a TV studio. I had spent a half hour reading about the meeting, which had been held by La Francophonie, the organization of French-speaking countries. This was not an organization whose activities I followed particularly closely—or at all—which explained why I wasn't aware of the goings-on at the meeting. But what had happened was pretty interesting. In examining recent hostilities between Israel and Lebanon, La Francophonie's membership had forwarded a resolution that expressed sympathy for the Lebanese victims of the violence without doing the same for their Israeli counterparts. It was the sort of unbalanced resolution I knew well from my days at the UN, criticizing Israel for its military actions—admittedly sometimes fairly—without putting them in the proper context of the constant threats it faced. At the UN, if it was a Security Council resolution, the United States would usually veto it. But the United States was obviously not a member of La Francophonie. And so, despite its meek reputation, it was Canada—led by its prime minister, Stephen Harper—that stepped in to block the passage of the resolution as it was written. Given that Canada is not usually a power player in international organizations, this was a surprising development, and I was expecting to be asked questions about its implications, as well as substantive ones about the underlying resolution.

Relatively confident that I would be able to discuss all this, I got to the studio and found that the only person there was a technician. I would be interviewed remotely by a host in a different studio, he explained, as he seated me in front of a large camera and put a headset on me.

"The producer there will give you all the instructions," he said as he left. "Just listen, and they'll talk to you soon."

I nodded and sat there, staring into the black screen in front of me. After a minute or so I heard the producer on the earphones.

"Mr. Levey," he said, "can you hear me?"

"Yes," I said.

"Good," he said. "This is a live interview, so are you ready?"

"Yes," I said.

"So in ten seconds," he continued, "we're going to talk about what happened today in Romania. And . . . ten . . ."

I gasped. What happened today in *Romania*? There must have been some mistake. I had no idea what had happened that day in Romania. In fact, I never had any idea of what happened in Romania.

"Nine . . ."

"Wait!" I said to the producer at the other end of the line. "What do you mean Romania? This was supposed to be about the Middle East meeting."

"Really?" he asked. "Hold on."

And then he was gone, and I was staring into the blackness of the monitor, continuing to count down where he had left off. Eight. Seven. Six.

"Five," I said to myself, convinced that in just another few seconds I would be live on television, being interviewed about what had happened in Romania—whatever that was.

"Well," I would expound, making it up as I went along, "the situation in Bucharest is complicated and nuanced. On the one hand, we have to be careful not to ascribe too much importance to the events there today, but on the other hand—"

Then I would rip my headpiece off and run out of the studio, screaming about having to go talk to my grocer. All on live television.

"Three," I continued counting. "Two . . ."

And just then the producer was back.

"The meeting of the Francophonie took place *in* Romania," he said.

And suddenly we were live and on the air. I managed to handle the interview without too much trouble, discussing the perceived imbalance of the Francophonie resolution. But anyone unfortunate enough to see that television appearance would have noticed that in my first seconds on the air my eyes were wide and, because my mouth was dry from nerves, I was licking my lips in a weird way that looked like I was trying to be seductive.

I recovered from my weird TV appearance and prepared to head off for AIPAC. But since my conversation with Stephen Walt was still swirling around in my head, I decided that I should balance it by talking to Abe Foxman, the national director of the Anti-Defamation League.

Foxman was one of Walt's sharpest critics and often an AIPAC ally. The ADL, a watchdog group that worked to fight anti-Semitism, was one of the pillars of the Jewish establishment in the United States—as active and influential in its realm as AIPAC was in its own. It didn't focus on Israel like AIPAC did, but given that modern manifestations of anti-Semitism were so frequently connected to Israel, they often waded into the Middle East debate as well.

Although Foxman was respected in many quarters, some—especially younger Jews—had serious misgivings about him. There were sometimes concerns, for example, that he was too eager to report incidents of bias or hate, having a tendency to cry wolf, and that this painted the Jewish community as a whole as reactionary.

"Is the problem of anti-Semitism in the U.S. getting better or worse?" I asked Foxman when I got him on the phone.

"The answer is yes," he said.

That's a very odd answer, I thought.

"In terms of attitudes," he said, "it has gotten better. In terms of classic anti-Semitic attitudes, forty years ago one-third of Americans were seriously infected by anti-Semitism. Today, anywhere from twelve to fourteen percent are. That's the good news. But the bad news is that that's still forty million Americans who are seriously infected with anti-Semitism.

"The other part of the bad news," he continued, "is that one-third continue to believe that the Jews killed Christ, and thirty percent believe that American Jews are more loyal to Israel than to the United States. So while things are generally better, the ingredients are still very serious, and there are still lingering concerns. Jews are seen as not loyal. They're seen as tied to Israel for better or worse."

This brought up a question in my mind. To what extent, I wondered, did Israeli policies, and the turmoil constantly swirling around Israel, actually *cause* anti-Semitism for Diaspora Jews? The State of Israel was founded as a refuge for Jews escaping endemic anti-Semitism, but so often today it seemed like anti-Semitism in the rest of the world was tied into concerns about Israel. Could Israel be making the problem worse for those of us living outside the country?

I tried to articulate this question to Foxman, trying to be careful to not sound anti-Israel myself but conscious of the fact that this ultrasensitive question could be construed as just that. Probably as a result of me trying to be delicate about it, though, I wasn't totally sure Foxman got what I was driving at. It was hard to tell from his response.

"Every time there is violence in the Middle East," he said, "it legitimizes the anti-Semitic platform."

It was time to dive in, I thought.

"Okay," I said. "My key question is how should I personally make peace in the Middle East?"

"Anybody can sit down for fifteen minutes and map out a peace settlement," he said immediately, and I considered telling him about my disastrous attempt at PeaceMaker, "and both you and I know what that would entail. A two-state solution. An exchange of land. A reasonable and rational approach to Jerusalem. And, of course, no right of return."

Most of this did indeed seem reasonable to me, though I knew that many Palestinians didn't see giving up their "right of return" as such a foregone conclusion. Also, while a "reasonable and rational approach to Jerusalem" sounded good, I knew the devil would be in the details on that one—and that reason and rationality were not exactly in large supply in the Middle East. Even if I personally mostly agreed with Foxman's plan, I knew plenty of people who would map out entirely different solutions. What seemed obvious to him was not necessarily so obvious to others.

I asked Foxman if he thought the U.S.-Israel dynamic was beginning to change a little, as Stephen Walt and others had suggested.

"It has only changed for those who want it to change," Foxman said. "It's only people who are trying to promote an agenda who try to say there is change. Those things that unite us as nations are so much greater than those that divide us."

This was a common rhetorical technique among Israel's supporters—pointing out the similarities and shared interests of the United States and Israel. I thought it had a lot of merit to it, but at the same time, I didn't think that if someone was trying to alter the relationship in order to foster a Middle East solution, they were necessarily trying to *divide* the two countries. Foxman was satisfied with the status quo, whereby the United States supported Israel's right to call the shots when it came to how quickly or slowly it wanted to move in the peace process, even if Israel's policies might be counterproductive for its own long-term survival.

"What do you think of Walt and Mearsheimer and their thesis?" I asked.

"It's abject nonsense," he said, "and part of the charge that we control the media. If it was true, they wouldn't have had the field day that they had. They accused me of not wanting to debate them, which is nonsense. They want to put themselves in victim mode."

Finally, I moved on to the divide between Foxman's ADL and younger Jews, who often weren't as engaged with the ADL's mission as their parents were, and who had sometimes taken aim at him and what they saw as his exaggerated focus on anti-Semitism. For example, one political cartoon drawn by the cartoonist Eli Valley and published in *The Jewish Daily Forward*, one of the Jewish establishment's most venerable publications, had depicted Foxman as a paranoid reactionary. It had him proclaiming, "It's like I always said—the best way to battle a stereotype is to embody it."

"Those sorts of people are just trying to get attention," he said. "I think it's fine, but I don't think they're a significant part of the American Jewish population. By all polls, Jews see anti-Semitism in the U.S. as a major concern. Those people make a point by appealing to the other side—to those without memory."

He explained that he was referring to the Holocaust, and that he believed that anyone with a real understanding of history wouldn't be so cavalier. For Foxman, as for a lot of Jewish people of his generation, the Holocaust would always stand as a powerful reminder that even a hint of anti-Semitism should not be countenanced, because there was no telling where it might lead.

I asked him specifically about Eli Valley's cartoon, and he answered, "I think what Eli Belly does is fine, but I would have thought the *Forward* was more serious . . ."

At this point, I stopped paying close attention, distracted, because I knew Eli personally.

Belly? I thought, as Foxman went on. *Did he just call Eli Valley 'Eli Belly'?*

*   *   *

I had a chance to tell Eli about this soon afterward, when I was visiting him in his apartment in the East Village. There were comics and comic-book art all over the walls, and books on everything from art to Jewish history. Beside a large window looking down at the traffic on Third Avenue, he had an easel set up, with a comic in progress. Valley was in his late thirties, but perhaps because he had a wild mop of curly hair and because of his colorful apartment and his irreverent cartoons, he seemed much younger.

"Is it okay if I call you Eli Belly too?" I asked.

"No," he said.

Moving on, I asked him what he thought about Foxman's assertion that he—and people like him—were just trying to get attention.

"In my comic about him, I was not making fun of the threat of anti-Semitism," he said. "Anti-Semitism in the Muslim world and Europe is dangerous. But I'm making fun of an individual who has built an entire career frightening Jews.

"It is in these people's vested interests to make the genuine threat of anti-Semitism bigger than it is. In the case of Foxman, he actually increases anti-Semitism. He's a walking stereotype. The whiney guy on TV who jumps on every case to complain about it—playing into the role of the paranoid Jew. Like a character from an earlier generation. Which, of course, he is."

For Eli, people like Foxman were not just oversensitive. They were actually insecure about their own places in the world and used their hypervigilance to bolster their senses of self-worth.

"Are you a self-hating Jew?" I asked.

"No, I'm a self-loving Jew," Eli said, "and I hate that term. I'm proud to be a Jew, but these people define themselves by pretending to psychoanalyze opponents—they are sniveling, insecure Jews who need to pump themselves up by insulting others."

Abe Foxman was hardly Eli's only target. He had drawn cartoons satirizing a wide range of figures, one of which in particular had set off a recent flood of controversy. The cartoon was about an imagined Evangelical tour of Israel, and had taken aim squarely at Evangelical Christian supporters of Israel, depicting them as bloodthirsty and anti-Semitic. Among other things, the Christians in the cartoon had said to the Israelis, "Excuse me, sir? Jew? Jesus is filled with nothing but love for you . . . and if you reject him, you'll face eternal torture, Judas!" and "Our pastor taught us that Hitler was fulfilling God's will." The cartoon had been bitterly attacked not just by Christian groups, but also by Jews and Israelis, and this criticism was discussed as far afield as a major Pakistani newspaper.

"Why did you think that one cartoon in particular raised the anger of so many people?" I asked him.

"Well," he said, "there were a lot of people in the Evangelical community who thought that I was depicting them as messianic lunatics hungering for the Apocalypse."

"Were you doing that?" I asked.

"Yes," he said.

Naturally, I asked Eli what he thought I should do to make Middle East Peace.

"A three-state solution," he said.

A three-state solution?

Various versions of the two-state solution were the ones most commonly floated around when people threw out ideas for peace, but what was a three-state solution?

There would be a moderate Jewish state and a moderate Palestinian state, Eli explained, and then there would be a third state where the extremists from *both* sides would live, fighting it out forever, as they seemed to wish to do. That third state would be called "Fundamentalistan."

Eli obviously wasn't being wholly serious, but he wasn't joking exactly either.

"It's humor born of frustration," he said. "The tragic truth here is that peace is impossible while each side has extremists subtly or overtly dictating policy."

Before ending our conversation, I went back to the topic of Foxman one more time, and asked Eli what he thought about Foxman's assertion that those who felt far removed from the Holocaust generation didn't see the world in the same way as their parents and grandparents did. He seemed to pretty much agree with him, but framed it differently.

"It's true we don't look at everything through the lens of the Holocaust," he said. "Those who grew up in its shadows do. And it skews everything for them."

In a sense, I thought, the way American Jews thought about the Middle East often turned on their own relationships to the Holocaust. The closer they felt to the Holocaust era, the more sensitive they generally were about Israel's security, and the more concerned they were about its short-term prospects. The question was whether keeping the Holocaust in sharp focus was useful or detrimental in contextualizing the Middle East today—or somewhere in between. Was it useful to include people in the debate who felt the Holocaust was merely history? Was it useful to include people still scarred by it?

If Valley and Foxman were in agreement on anything, it was that the rift between their two worldviews was generational in nature.

And for me personally, this rift was about to hit home.

Just after I met with Eli, I got a call from my uncle. Obviously, he knew about my first book and what I was up to now, and in the call it became quickly evident that he wasn't particularly happy about either of them. At first the conversation went okay, but when I made some joke about the Israeli settlers possibly planning to colonize Japan, it took an unpleasant turn.

"You know," he said, a rougher tone entering his voice, "you just don't get it, do you?

"Get what?" I asked.

"You don't get what Israel means to us, to people who remember when we didn't know if it would survive. To people whose families were murdered by the Germans. You just don't understand what it means to us who grew up after the Holocaust—when it felt like it was our only lifeline."

This was a bit overwhelming, especially since it felt like it had come out of nowhere. I was pretty sure that I did in fact have a fairly good understanding of the importance of Israel to Diaspora Jews as an emotional homeland and as a life raft in case things abroad started tending a little toward, well, 1939. I probably didn't feel it as viscerally as did Jews of older generations, or as did Jews in countries where it was still a little dicey to be open about one's Jewish identity. But that didn't mean I didn't "get it."

Besides, Israelis themselves often made light of their difficult situation. The country had a lot of black humor. For example, when they were off duty, the Israel Defense Forces' combat engineers—the troops charged with using explosives to blow up structures in war zones—sometimes wore T-shirts with their unit's name on them and pictures of soldiers who were smilingly showing off their missing limbs. But even besides the fact that Israelis were themselves no strangers to humor satirizing their difficult situation, my joke that had incited the negative turn in our conversation had been about the settlements. It hadn't been about Israel's right to exist or about suicide bombers or anything of that kind. To the extent that the settlements delayed peace, I thought, they were a threat to Israel's long-term viability. If my uncle cared about Israel as deeply as he claimed, then wouldn't he be as concerned about them as me?

"Look," I said, "I've ordered some underwear that should solve everything."

"It's all a big joke to you, isn't it?" he asked.

And then he hung up on me.

CHAPTER FIVE

A Very Dangerous Suburban Dad

The AIPAC conference was held at the massive Washington Convention Center, and as I approached the building, it occurred to me that to some, it might seem like I was walking into the belly of the beast. AIPAC was so maligned in certain quarters that even an event at such a high-profile venue would hold a whiff of conspiracy for them. This was, after all, the heart of Stephen Walt and his colleague John Mearsheimer's "Israel Lobby."

More than six thousand AIPAC delegates from all over the country had converged on Washington, and to accommodate them, there were hordes of volunteers and staff, all working together seamlessly. I made my way through all this to pick up my press credentials, and then went to the main conference hall.

It was huge and full of elaborate lights and sound equipment. An enormous screen stood at the front of the room behind the stage, flanked by large Israeli and American flags. I went to the area reserved for the media, and pretty soon an AIPAC staffer arrived and introduced himself as Josh Block, AIPAC's spokesman.

Josh and I had spoken on the phone a number of times when I had been writing Middle East news stories, and in person he was as charming, polished, and likable as I'd expected.

"What do you think?" he asked, indicating the hall.

"Very impressive," I said and meant it.

Meanwhile, hundreds of AIPAC delegates continued to file in. Alongside the rank-and-file members, there was a section roped off for VIPs, where there were dozens of congressmen and senators, diplomats and former diplomats, and even defense and intelligence officials, as well as some of the biggest figures in Washington's lobbying circles and the American Jewish community.

Over the next couple of days, all of us listened to what seemed like an endless stream of speeches by politicians, activists, and pundits. Some of them were delivered in the giant main hall, others in smaller breakout sessions. But all of them had the same set of themes—the sanctity of the relationship between the United States and Israel and the importance of maintaining Israel's security in the face of threats like Iran.

The viewpoints expressed ranged along a spectrum, from extremely hawkish to relatively moderate. But all of them were, at least generally speaking, reasonable. Even at the most hawkish, when the speakers prioritized maintaining Israel's military edge above all else, urged for military action against Iran and ascribed absolutely no value to trying to foster better relations with the Arab world as a way of building security, they still were not spewing hate speech against Arabs or Muslims or accusing the U.S. government of being motivated by anti-Semitism. I didn't personally agree with a lot of what was said, but very little of it was completely wild or irrational like some of the commentary that came to me from other sources. AIPAC's brass was careful to keep things grounded and relatively mainstream.

But the same could not be said for the grassroots AIPAC members I found myself surrounded by—and, at one point, pursued by.

I was in the convention center's little coffee shop between sessions, when I spotted a woman I recognized but couldn't place. We made eye contact, and she started heading over. Only as she reached me did I remember that we'd met at a mutual friend's birthday party in New York. We had spoken just a little then, but she had seemed nice enough and levelheaded.

Not so in the context of the AIPAC conference.

"So you're a journalist now," she said.

"Sort of," I told her, which just seemed easier than telling her the whole story.

"Well, are you like every other journalist?" she asked. "Only able to hate on Israel constantly?"

"No," I said, a little taken aback by the generalization. "Of course not."

"Well, I don't know what's wrong with the rest of them," she went on. "Don't they realize that Israel is our only ally in the Middle East? They're all just a bunch of Jew-haters."

"Um . . ." I said, thinking, *Can I go back to my seat now?*

I knew lots of journalists, and counted some of them as my closest friends. None of the ones I knew were "Jew-haters." In fact, it often felt like the majority of them *were* Jews. I wasn't going to mention that, because I knew the inevitable response would be that they were self-hating Jews.

"Well," I said, "I don't think they're *all* like that."

"Have you *read* the *New York Times*?" she asked. "Have you *seen* CNN?"

I considered telling her that I had never heard of either, but thought better of it.

"Uh, yeah," I said, just wanting to leave the conversation. "I have."

"Well, then you know," she continued, pointing at my chest, "how much they have it in for Israel."

I had encountered hundreds of people who held this sort of view. They thought that when mainstream American news organizations covered the Middle East conflict, the organizations were consistently and demonstrably biased against Israel. This would, of course, have been baffling to the average citizen of Europe or the Arab world, who believed the precise opposite, but it was taken as almost a given among a certain demographic of American supporters of Israel.

When they reported a story about an Israeli military maneuver against the Palestinians, for example, the people in this demographic argued that the context of the maneuver—Palestinian aggression against Israel—was never fully conveyed. To them, reporters approached the situation with a predisposition, or even an eagerness, to criticize Israel.

I really didn't want to get into this with this woman, who was proving far more belligerent than I remembered. My own opinion was that, for the most part, American journalists did *not* "have it in for Israel." Many journalists were relatively liberal, and probably wouldn't see eye to eye with most of the AIPAC crowd, but they very seldom misreported facts to push a particular agenda.

"I think everyone at CNN and the *New York Times*," she said, "simply hates Jews. That's all there is to it."

"I'm going to go back to my seat now," I said, walking in that direction.

"Okay," she said, following me.

No, I wanted to say, *I mean I'm going to go back to my seat now, and I would like you to stay here.*

But I just walked away briskly, hoping that I could somehow outpace her. As she sped up to keep up with me, my instinct was to actually run, but I knew that would have looked a little weird.

"I'm part of an organization," she said as we near-jogged along together through the crowds of AIPAC delegates, many of whom were looking at us oddly because of the speed at which we were walking, "that organizes to complain to media organizations about their biased coverage. Maybe you'd like to get involved?"

I definitely did not want to get involved. And luckily, just as she asked this last question, I reached the press area and leapt behind the cord that roped it off from the rest of the crowd. I knew it was obnoxious of me, and a bunch of the journalists were giving me an odd look because of my running leap into the media area, but I didn't care. When we said good-bye and she walked off, I was grateful for that divide.

* * *

At a luncheon event the next day, I found myself longing for another divide to hide behind. I was sitting beside a middle-aged couple with their daughter, who looked about fifteen. They were from a suburb of New York City, and they were Jewish. The father of the family, who was immediately beside me, was a psychiatrist. And so by most measures, it felt like they were from the same East Coast Jewish world with which I was familiar.

But when we got past the introductions and small talk—during which the psychiatrist dad casually mentioned that one of the magazines I wrote for was "only for Leftists"—it became increasingly clear that while that world I knew was predominantly liberal, these people were anything but.

"The Democrats," he said, "want to sell Israel down the river."

And when we started talking a bit more about the issues themselves and the question of Iran came up, he thought the idea of not attacking the Islamic Republic as soon as possible was ridiculous and short-sighted. The mullahs were bent on Israel's destruction, and the only thing to do was to take them out. With no time to spare, no mercy, and definitely no time for diplomacy or negotiation.

"That would just be a delaying tactic on their end," he told me.

He had a lot more to say too. None of the Palestinians truly wanted peace, he contended, because the only thing that mattered to them was that the Jews were driven into the ocean. The only solution was complete destruction, not only of the Palestinians, but also of the Arabs in the other countries surrounding Israel—

the peace treaties with Jordan and Egypt were just Arab ruses, after all. And anyone in Europe or the United States who did not support this course of action was likely just an anti-Semite who wished Hitler had finished what he started—a logically peculiar but all-too-frequent reflexive jump for so many in the far right fringe among Israel's supporters.

All this in soft, calm tones.

Then, after talking about how it wouldn't be such a bad thing if Saudi Arabia was carpet bombed, he asked me, "What's your email address?"

I supported Israel as much as the next guy. Just, well, not as much as the next guy at this particular conference. And the single-minded focus of them all, even the more moderate ones, had the effect of repelling me. It also made me feel more at home with the journalists, who circulated through the crowds like anthropologists in some exotic foreign land, returning to the press area now and then for a break from it all.

At one point, though, I felt some doubt about where my allegiances truly lay. I was going into one of the conference rooms to watch a panel discuss ways to use financial pressure to force Iran to give up its nuclear ambitions when I noticed that the pushy friend-of-a-friend from earlier was coming in behind me. Before she saw me, I quickly ducked behind a very round man, who was standing on the side of the room, holding a clipboard.

I was unnaturally close to him, so that I could use him for cover, and he looked back at me questioningly. I just smiled at him and nodded, but he didn't seem to like this, and he stepped to the side to get some space. Unfortunately, this was the precise moment that my friend-of-a-friend was passing by, and so I had no choice but to step closer to the large man again to maintain my cover.

"Dude!" he said, with a hard edge to his voice. "What's your problem?"

But she'd walked on now, and so with a quick awkward smile at the large man, I slipped away to the back of the room, where I took the first seat I found.

There were at least a hundred people in the room, but it so happened that I recognized the woman next to me from the press tables. I hadn't spoken to her there, but I'd seen her sitting with a cameraman, who was now standing behind the chairs, setting up a video camera on a tripod.

She noticed the press ID I was wearing and smiled.

"You're a reporter?" she asked, with a European accent I couldn't identify right away.

"Sort of," I told her, and immediately I saw a small but unmissable change in her body language. It was as if she felt more comfortable with me now that she knew I wasn't there as a regular attendee. As if she could relate to me now.

I noticed, meanwhile, that the round man was still giving me a stern look, and I turned to face her directly so I could avoid him.

"So what do you think of all this?" she asked me, sweeping a hand across the scene. She looked like she was overwhelmed.

I shrugged, and it was not a gesture with no meaning. I really wasn't sure what I thought of it. And something about her obvious unease with the scene had the sudden and odd effect of making *me* uncomfortable with her.

"Oh, I don't know," I said. "Quite a production, huh?"

"Yes, it's shocking." She nodded. "These people frighten me."

And suddenly, almost despite myself, I had the urge to defend them.

What do you mean? I wanted to demand. *What are you trying to say?*

And I also thought: *Is that a German accent?*

I rejected my uncle's hyperbolic reactions, and I didn't think that any new Holocaust was in the offing. But anti-Semitism in Europe—real anti-Semitism—was a growing problem, and despite my best efforts at being liberal, modern, and forward looking, I couldn't help but think that if I were a German speaker I might be a little careful around Jewish-related issues.

In our daily lives and our worldviews, I probably had far more in common with her than with the majority of the AIPAC delegates. But something about her, about her criticizing in her German accent, made me wonder if, deep down, I didn't share a little bit of my uncle's Holocaust preoccupation.

Even as I was trying to understand my own positions on the issues, I was only getting increasingly confused.

In the next break, I retreated to a room that had been set aside for journalists to make phone calls and use computers. There, I called Abby to let her know how things were going.

"I hid behind a fat man to avoid running into a crazy woman," I told her.

"That's great," she said, not sounding especially impressed. "Good job."

"Also," I said, "I met a suburban psychiatrist who wants to carpet bomb Saudi Arabia."

"Great job," she said, clearly not paying attention. "Keep up the good work."

After updating Abby, I decided to check my email.

I logged in and was delighted to see that there was a response to the email I had sent to Wayne the foul-mouthed Brit before leaving for the conference.

All the email said was: "Is this about the Israel thing?"

Of course it is! I wanted to yell. If there was any time I was surrounded by the "Israel nutters," as Wayne had put it, it was right now. Could he possibly think that his ranting lecture in the restaurant that day had discouraged me from doing this?

"Yes," I wrote back. It was about the "Israel thing." And I could really use his help.

There was a lot of buzz at the conference about a statement that presidential candidate Obama had recently made. "Nobody is suffering more than the Palestinian people," he had said, and this had turned into a major mark against him in the eyes of the AIPAC crowd. At the conference, there were even people passing around flyers to let others know that he had said it, interpreting this comment to mean that he was an anti-Israel Palestinian sympathizer. In fact, the aspersions cast against Obama by those renegade AIPAC members—they were not sanctioned by the AIPAC leadership— were just a small part of a much larger effort at work to use the Middle East conflict to discredit his candidacy. Emails were circulated alleging that he was an anti-Semite, an extremist Muslim, and an Israel hater. These emails were directed at the Jewish community, particularly at the older Jews living in key electoral battlegrounds like Florida. As a result, many older Jews were starting to be concerned about Obama's plans for Israel, and a rift was forming between them and their children and grandchildren, who were enthusiastic supporters of the young senator from Illinois.

Even during the Democratic primaries, the Middle East debate was a battle zone in the war between Barack Obama's and Hillary Clinton's camps. Clinton, because of her tight relations with Israel and the American Jewish community, was perceived by many as a safer bet for those deeply concerned about maintaining American support for Israel. Obama, they argued, was just too big of a risk when it came to the safety of the Jewish state. Polls showed that younger Jewish voters were more likely to give Obama the benefit of the doubt on Israel or to not prioritize the Israel issue as much as their parents and grandparents did, while older Jews held the issue as crucial and were hesitant to trust Obama.

It wasn't on the Middle East issue per se, but this generational divide had even arisen in my own family—in a totally unexpected way.

During the primaries, I answered my phone and heard a young child's voice saying "Bama" excitedly. It took me a moment to realize that it was Jonah, the son of Abby's sister, Melissa. He was not quite two years old and was trying to say, "Go, Obama!"

His parents were not happy about this. They were enthusiastic supporters of Hillary Clinton and had told both their sons—the older one was four years old—that the family would be supporting Clinton. All was well and good until Ben, the four-year-old, saw the two candidates in action on TV, shook his head, and said, "No. I like him."

It wasn't long before his younger brother, following his lead, joined the Obama camp as well—and began making phone calls to my house to raise support for his chosen candidate.

On the day of their primary in Virginia, they were on the way to the polling station when the four-year-old had a scream-ing tantrum. He was wildly angry about two things. First, he had discovered that children were not allowed to vote ("Not fair!"), and second, his parents were still planning to vote for Clinton.

Both kids were upset about this turn of events. The next day, of course, my nephews were pleased to hear that their candidate had won their state's primary, despite their parents' obtuseness. Some time later, though, Ben saw Clinton on the television, and said, "She's done. Throw her in the trash."

Political free speech was one thing, his mother thought, but this was going too far. So he was given a time-out. And he was reprimanded again later because he called John McCain "stupid." That was not nice, his mother told him, but added that he was allowed to call McCain "old."

I was sitting beside both kids one day when CNN showed a clip of Obama speaking about education. At one point he said the word "children," and Ben exploded with delight.

"He's talking about us!" he yelled, while his little brother bounced up and down on the couch, clapping. "He's talking *to* us!"

On the other side of the room, Abby's sister shook her head in disbelief and fatigue.

"He's talking to us!" the little one chimed in as well now, copying his brother. "He's talking to us!"

And before the primaries had ended, the two of them came up with a strategy they wanted Obama to employ.

"On TV," they said earnestly to anyone who would listen, "he should always be holding puppies and kittens."

Amid the speeches by politicians, Israeli officials, and Jewish leaders at the AIPAC conference, there was one moment that stood out for me. Pastor John Hagee, founder of Christians United for Israel, the preeminent Christian Zionist organization in America, took the podium at one of the gala events—and I knew within seconds that this was going to be what I would remember best.

Hagee was an expert orator. As a former speechwriter, I found myself wishing that I had written for someone with such a commanding presence, who was able to captivate an audience like he did. And even though he spoke of the Middle East conflict in biblical terms, and I was a total nonbeliever—in Judaism, let alone Evangelical Christianity—he definitely had my attention throughout.

"The sleeping giant of Christian Zionism has awoken!" he roared. "Israel lives! Israel lives! Shout it from the mountaintops! Israel lives!"

The battle between the Israel–United States alliance and the

Iranian-Hezbollah-Hamas axis was cast in apocalyptic terms. The Iranian regime represented the armies of the devil, and the Jews of Israel represented the children of light who would triumph in a final battle that would bring on salvation.

As I looked around me, it was clear that the crowd was rapt. They cheered him on as he roared about divine covenants and invoked his Christian doctrines about Jerusalem. This was all the more amazing given that the vast majority of the audience was Jewish, and that many of them were even Orthodox Jews.

As far as I had always understood the theology of the Hagees of the world, the fate of the Jews in their prophesy wasn't all that rosy. In order to bring about the Rapture, his followers worked to encourage Jewish immigration to Israel and to defend Israel's security. But eventually, when the End Times finally came, the options for the Jews boiled down to: convert or die.

So the warmth with which this primarily Jewish audience greeted the pastor's words was startling, but the end of the world wasn't really their concern at this point. Their concern was the security of Israel, and in Hagee's hawkishness to the Jewish state's enemies and the clout he wielded with the Evangelical Christian voting block in the United States, they saw him as a crucial ally.

Indeed, the upcoming presidential election was looming behind the whole AIPAC event, and at one point during Hagee's speech, I overheard a delegate nearby me whisper something interesting.

"I'm going to vote for *him*," he said.

* * *

As the conference came to a close, many attendees were going off to do something I couldn't take part in. Before returning to their homes, they were set to make a concrete contribution to the AIPAC mission. During the conference, they had been attending "lobbying labs," in which they had learned the most effective ways to persuade their elected representatives of the wisdom of the AIPAC case, and now they were going to go to a series of meetings with their senators and congressmen to implement the skills they had learned. An army of persuaders.

The talking points they were armed with included the cultural similarities between the United States and Israel, Israel's role in the "war on terror," and the idea that Israel sincerely strived for peace while the Palestinians refused it.

But they had also been told that part of the message they needed to convey was that each of them represented thousands more back home who hadn't been able to make it to Washington. This was probably true. Thousands of more letter writers. Thousands of more voters. Thousands of more campaign donors. Millions of more dollars.

No matter how off-kilter some of these people seemed, no politician was going to turn his back on all that. Here, in many ways, was the power of AIPAC in real life—the thousands of people it represented and the sway they held over their elected representatives when it came to making Middle East policy. Whether that influence was for better or worse depended on who you asked, but there was no denying it.

As for me, I was headed back to my apartment, hoping that a certain package was waiting there.

CHAPTER SIX

"I Should Believe That You Don't Surprising"

I came home and was disappointed to find that my PeaceMaker boxer shorts had still not arrived. Also, I had not yet heard back again from Wayne. The only email in my in-box was from someone who called himself "Lion Claw."

I had no idea who Lion Claw was or what he wanted from me, but it was clear he hadn't chosen me randomly, because the email was about the Middle East. And, inevitably, it was full of inflammatory and extremist rhetoric. At first I just wrote it off as another crazy emailer, but then something occurred to me: the email had been sent to my personal address, not my website address. Whoever Lion Claw was, he knew me.

Then I put it together. This desktop war hero was the psychiatrist I sat next to at the AIPAC conference. The one with the wife and child who lived in the suburbs of New York. In the email he came across as even more zealous than he had in person, and I got the sinking feeling that I would be hearing a lot more from him.

Of course, by now I was used to being flooded by strange emails and letters. They had been coming in steadily since my book had come out, and before that I had gotten them because of my journalism. A man named Ted Collins, for example, bombarded my in-box almost daily with various right-wing screeds. Several times a week, apparently, it was imperative that I knew what Ted Collins thought about the Middle East.

Before *that*, though, I had received them at the Israeli prime minister's office and UN Mission, where my job had sometimes included fielding them. In those days, one particularly frequent sender had been someone named Harold C Funk, who called himself The Voice of the Voiceless. On reading his notes, I had always thought that if Mr. Funk was their only voice, the voiceless might be better off just staying silent. One of his had read in part along these lines:

Dear Head of Nation,

Is there some reason you are abusing dogs? Is there some reason you are using marijuana? Is there some reason you are using heroin? Is there some reason you are using alcohol? Is there some reason you are using nuclear weapons on my family? Is there some reason that you spy on everyone on Earth?

Peace,
Harold C Funk
The Voice of the Voiceless

"I Should Believe That You Don't Surprising"

The letters I got from other people back then were sometimes sinister, sometimes crazy, and sometimes even charming. But always a little odd. Often, I had ended up with letters like:

Hello diplomatic official of ISRAEL,

Let me introduce myself. I am university student in South Korea. I am 26 year old and name is KIM CHANG LEE. KIM is my family name. CHANG LEE is second name. So I want that you calling me LEE.

My professor set a homework to student who is attending his lecture. The homework is that researching activity of any country's mission to the United Nations. So I choosed your country because your country made it patriotic motto to do. South Korea is small country. But we do not have power as strong as Israel. So I think about that Israel is very good model of South Korean developing. So I do not hesitate to pay Israel choosing. I feel keenly the necessity of your helping. I swear! I only use your information to scientific research.

I should believe that you don't surprising.

KIM CHANG LEE

Sitting in one of my favorite bars one day with my friends Jane and P.J., I told them about all the odd emails. About Ted Collins and about the newest addition, Lion Claw.

They were laughing at the situation, but I was eager to get into why I had asked them to meet with me. Jane was Jewish and

P.J. was Palestinian, and they seemed to be a very happy couple. Sure, they lived in New York and didn't have to actually deal with the situation in the Middle East on a granular level, but I still thought they might have something valuable to contribute to the discussion.

P.J.'s father was actually a renowned Palestinian intellectual, and P.J. himself was fairly deeply involved with discussions about the Middle East. Jane was less engaged with the Middle East situation, but I knew she was still fairly attentive. I was curious to know what their interactions were like when the issue came up.

"Well, mostly it doesn't," Jane told me. "And when it does, we usually pretty much agree."

"What about your families?" I asked.

Both of them smiled, and I sensed there was something to be said about this.

"It was maybe a little bit of an issue at the beginning," P.J. said. "But I think they're all used to it now."

Jane nodded in agreement.

"Is it comfortable?" I asked, and Jane shrugged.

"Well, at your cousin's bat mitzvah—" P.J. began.

"Oh, yeah," Jane said. "That."

Apparently, at Jane's younger cousin's bat mitzvah, P.J. had felt especially uneasy. The temple where the ceremony was held had an Israeli flag on display, and at one point during the service, a prayer was said for the State of Israel—far from uncommon in American synagogues.

"I had always thought being a Jew in America was just a matter of religion," P.J. told me, "and was not necessarily connected to Israel. But suddenly there was that prayer, and I thought, Wow. This is definitely not something I can be a part of."

"Really?" Jane asked him. "It was that prayer that got to you so much?"

P.J. nodded, and for a moment they seemed to forget that I was even there and began discussing how P.J. had felt extremely uneasy at the ceremony, alienated, separate, and hurt, with Jane realizing dimensions of this that she hadn't realized at the time. It was a poignant scene, and I felt like I was intruding on something personal.

When we got back on track, I asked P.J. what his perspective on solving the conflict was. Did he support two states for the two peoples? Or would he prefer one single state?

"I would *prefer* it," P.J. said, "if Israel and Palestine turned into the U.S.: a single multiethnic, multireligious nation. That's the more civilized, evolved, and advanced option. I would much rather have that than have two states defined in part by their ethno-religious identity. But what kind of solution we have is secondary to me. I am in favor of whatever solution has the best odds of giving everyone basic human rights, and I think that a fair two-state solution is more likely to produce that result, because it is more likely to get buy-in from both sides."

I looked at Jane, and she was nodding. They seemed to be on the same page.

* * *

Speaking to Jane and P.J. reminded me that I had been wanting to speak to a comedian named Ray Hanania for some time. Hanania, I had heard, was Palestinian and was married to a Jewish woman.

So when he next performed in town, I went to his show, and found that this relationship actually provided a lot of fodder for his routine. At their wedding, he said, they had Jews on one side and Arabs on the other, which meant that instead of a bridal party marching down the aisle, they had to have UN peacekeepers. He also joked that when his Jewish wife wasn't around, he referred to his young son Aaron as Abdelleh, meaning "servant of Allah."

Hanania told the crowd that he saw us not as audience members so much as "potential hostages," and that when he had flown on El Al, he had known it was an Israeli airline because he got up to use the bathroom and found a little sign that said "Occupied." Also, he said, when he returned to his seat, there was someone else sitting in it, and Alan Dershowitz suddenly arrived to explain why that was fair.

I wanted to see what he had to say when he wasn't joking around quite so much, and later I arranged to have a conversation with him.

"Do you and your wife have totally aligned views on the Middle East?" I asked him, wondering if they were like Jane and P.J. "Or do you have disagreements?"

"We have serious disagreements on it," he said. "She has a knee-jerk reaction to always defend Israel, and while I try to be evenhanded, I often reflexively feel for the Palestinians. But when we engage substantively on the topic, we often agree."

It was interesting, I thought, how often I found that when

people who might have knee-jerk reactions to the Middle East situation actually talked rationally through the issues, their views came out less rigid and more nuanced.

Hanania and I proceeded to get into a conversation about humor, and whether it was a way of dealing with the Middle East situation. Unsurprisingly, we quickly found some common ground.

"It's not the answer," he said, "but it can help build bridges. Sometimes humor is exactly what people need in times of conflict. It gets them to chill out and overcome fear without realizing it."

I thought there was definitely something to this—to the idea that humor could help foster an atmosphere conducive to peace by reducing tensions, putting people at ease, and overcoming rifts. Obviously, it wasn't the solution by itself, but maybe humor had a role to play in my own endeavors.

Speaking of tons of laughs, soon after that I heard some intriguing new information about the world of Washington DC lobbying.

"Well, I hear AIPAC may have some competition soon," a Middle East activist told me. "You didn't hear it from me, but there is an alliance forming against it."

Now, I'm getting somewhere, I thought. *Hushed conversations, secret alliances.*

"What do you mean?" I asked.

"I can't say," she told me, but she did give me the names of people she thought might give me information. When I called them later, most were reluctant to talk, but some gave me pieces of the puzzle, and the outlines of the story began to fall into place.

Several dovish Israel-oriented groups had been meeting about possibly joining forces to influence American policy. These little groups had been around for decades, but compared to AIPAC, they were ineffectual and lacked resources. It seemed that things were about to change, though, because even though the groups had coordinated activities before, this time there was the possibility of an added ingredient. Cash.

George Soros, the international financier, was in talks with them about funding an initiative that would bring them together and allow them to have more sway. Soros had long been an active donor to left-wing and pacificist causes, and although the Middle East had never been one of his focus areas, it seemed that he was interested in making a difference in the troubled region. The nascent alliance had even been nicknamed "the Soros initiative." Nothing might come of all this, I thought, or maybe something huge might.

I would have to go back down to Washington to find out.

But before I went back down to DC, there was something I had to take care of. It had been a while now since I had ordered my PeaceMaker boxer shorts, and there was no sign that they would be arriving anytime soon. But since they had come to take on an almost symbolic importance to me, I wasn't comfortable continuing without them. It was time to complain.

I called the company that actually manufactured and shipped

the boxer shorts for PeaceMaker, but wasn't able to get any information about when I would receive them. So I had no choice but to get in touch with the people of PeaceMaker themselves.

The guy I reached was an executive who dealt with high-level business decisions, and he seemed a little surprised to be contacted directly about a pair of wayward underwear. But I dropped the name of Asi Burak—the inventor of PeaceMaker—and mentioned that I had recently interviewed him, and the executive agreed to personally look into my order.

Hopefully I'd get my underwear soon.

But I'd have to go back to DC without them.

"Peace just can't come from the bloody region itself without American support," said Daniel Levy, one of the main architects of the movement to provide an alternative to AIPAC, when I met him in his office in DC. "Nothing will happen if it's bloody left to them. And the policies in place are unproductive."

Levy was English—hence all the "bloody" this and "bloody" that—but he was also Israeli. After graduating from Cambridge, he immigrated to Israel, where he eventually became a special advisor in the prime minister's office and a peace negotiator during the heady days of the 1990s. Just recently, he had moved to Washington to take a position at the New America Foundation, a left-leaning think tank not far from the White House.

"On issues where we disagree with AIPAC, we'll feel free to make our opinions known," he said. "You can think of it as giving cover to senators and congressmen who—"

Just then his phone rang, and he picked it up and had a quick conversation in English before saying good-bye in Hebrew.

"My wife," he said when he put down the phone.

"You speak to her in English?" I asked. He had told me earlier that she had immigrated to Israel from the former Soviet bloc.

"Yes," he said, "usually."

The whole issue of Israel and identity was confusing, I thought. Here was an English guy who had taken Israeli citizenship and served in the Israeli government, but had married a woman from within the former Soviet bloc whom he had met in the Middle East. They spoke English to each other, and now they were living in the United States, and he was playing a part in trying to influence U.S. foreign policy. None of that seemed to hang together quite right.

In a way, Levy had already walked the same terrain I was trying to traverse. In 2003, along with the Israeli politician Yossi Beilin, he had been one of the primary Israeli architects of what was called the Geneva Initiative. A group of Israelis, none of them sanctioned by the Israeli government, had met with a group of similarly unauthorized Palestinians and had hammered out what they considered a workable peace plan. Levy had been the plan's lead drafter.

The plan's solution to the conflict had provided for two states, with the Israelis giving up most of the West Bank and part of Jerusalem and removing almost all of their settlements. In exchange, the Palestinians gave up any further claims on the land and limited the exercise of their "right of return" to Israel-proper to a nominal number of returning refugees. It was a clear, rational approach that seemed to appeal to moderates on both sides.

But neither the actual Israeli government nor the actual Palestinian government were particularly pleased about this development—and neither one was going to honor what was only an agreement in fantasyland.

So what was the point in the Geneva Initiative? Was it to raise awareness about the possibility of agreement? Was it just to get attention? Or did its participants really think that what they had devised might be implemented?

From talking to Levy and reading press coverage of the event, it seemed to me to be a combination of these elements. It had been a big, bold move to take a situation that seemed trapped in gridlock and shake it up—much like his current project to change the face of U.S.-Israeli relations.

Later, I went to visit Daniel Levy's main ally in the quest to create an alternative to AIPAC. Unlike Levy, Jeremy Ben-Ami was not only American but had a long history of working in the institutions of American government. He served as an advisor in the Clinton White House and as policy director in Howard Dean's presidential campaign.

But once again, identities were slippery things. When I had initially been looking into the Soros initiative, and had heard about Jeremy, one of the other players in the movement had mentioned to me that he was descended from right-wing Israeli aristocracy. His father had fought alongside Menachem Begin in the Irgun, the prestate Zionist militia that many people, including many other Jews at the time, had considered terrorists. Going into my meeting with him, I wondered if any of that righteous zeal had been passed down to him.

When I met him, though, he didn't strike me as the progeny of a ruthless nationalist fighter so much as the type of bookish policy wonk that is as at home in DC as cherry blossoms in the springtime and gangland shootings the rest of the year.

But more than anyone, more than Daniel Levy or their other allies, and more than moneyman George Soros, this was the guy who was aiming to change the way Washington handled the situation in the Middle East.

"In a way," he told me after I explained to him why I myself was in DC, "we're both trying to do the same thing. We're both trying to make peace."

I nodded. He was right.

And then he added: "So I guess we're in a race. Let's see who can do it first."

I raised an eyebrow and looked at him suspiciously. Was that a challenge?

He smiled and nodded. I smiled too, but a little reluctantly. Did I now have some competition? I stopped smiling, and nodded in a way that I imagined was challenging. He nodded right back.

Okay, I thought, *enough of this standoff. Let's get down to business.*

"If your father were alive," I said, "what would he think about what you're doing?"

Ben-Ami smiled a different sort of grin and leaned back a bit.

"On the one hand," he said, "he'd be thrilled that I'm committed to finishing building the Jewish homeland. But on the other, he'd probably disagree with how I'm doing it."

I thought this was a good answer, but I wondered if it was accurate. In a nutshell, what Ben-Ami was trying to do was to have the United States pressure Israel to make concessions its democratically elected government was hesitant to do. I didn't know Ben-Ami's father, of course, but could someone committed to the hard-line philosophy of the Irgun—the organization that was responsible for one full-scale massacre of Arab civilians and a slew of other incidents that resulted in the spilling of innocent blood—ever really appreciate that approach?

"How did you get involved in this issue?" I asked. "And how'd you end up coming at it from this angle?"

He told me it began when he had been the deputy campaign manager for Mark Green when Green had been running for mayor of New York. During the campaign, Green had attended a fund-raiser for the dovish group Americans for Peace Now, and had been attacked for it in the New York Jewish community. A consultant had been brought in to handle the damage and had advised the Green campaign that their candidate should renounce Americans for Peace Now, return the money they had donated to his campaign, and go to Israel on a trip organized by AIPAC.

Ben-Ami had been surprised that right-wing Middle East politics had infiltrated a municipal election, and had thought, *Something has to change.* This had mobilized him to begin thinking about how to help bring about that change. And it had eventually led him to where he was now: trying to shake up the situation by bringing about an atmosphere where a more diverse set of views, including supporting dovish strategies, was tolerated.

But there was a powerful infrastructure determined to stop him, and he knew the road ahead was a rocky one.

I decided to call a close AIPAC ally I knew and ask him what he thought of the new movement that Daniel Levy and Jeremy Ben-Ami were leading.

"It's a lot of nothing," he said. "The same wine in a new bottle. These people have been around for years, with different names in different groups, but it's the same discredited ideology they're trying to push now, and nobody serious cares at all."

But wasn't the key difference now the money of one of the most powerful financiers in the world?

"Soros's involvement actually hurts their case," he said. "He's always been anti-Israel and anti-America, and most congressmen aren't going to touch something he's involved in with a ten-foot pole."

"Is AIPAC at all nervous?" I asked.

He laughed hard at this, and although the laugh sounded genuine, I wondered if maybe it was a bit forced. Was the idea really *that* funny?

"Not in the slightest," he told me. "What this group of fringe people are trying to do is a nonissue. Everyone knows that the voice to go to on Israel is AIPAC, and it's going to stay that way."

I wondered if he was protesting too much. Was he actually worried?

"You know what the truth is?" he went on. "It's that these people are just a bunch of bitter, marginalized misfits who are pissed off because they are ignored by the mainstream of American society and are just trying desperately to feel relevant."

And, in fact, just after I got back home, I heard some news that was going to put a damper on Daniel Levy and Jeremy Ben-Ami's plans. George Soros had pulled out of the Soros initiative, taking by far the biggest donation to the initiative with him and putting the whole thing on ice.

"But why?" I asked one of the people involved.

"I don't think he was ever fully committed to it," he said. "And I think he was uncomfortable with the amount of attention his part in the whole thing was getting."

It seemed like, for now at least, the door had closed on the alternative to AIPAC. I wasn't positive that Levy and Ben-Ami's dovish ideas had merit, but I was disappointed that they hadn't gotten a chance to give them a try.

It was not long after that that I heard about the online suicide bombing.

An employee of a Jewish nonprofit mentioned it to me matter-of-factly shortly after I heard about Soros's departure from the new movement.

"What the hell is an online suicide bombing?" I asked.

She explained that it had happened in Second Life, the virtual world where real people created imaginary characters and ran imaginary lives for them.

"The Jewish community of Second Life is still reeling from it," she said.

Hold on, hold on, hold on, I thought. *The Jewish community of Second Life?*

What was this wacko blathering on about?

And that is how I began to discover that in the Middle East getting entangled in local politics—as Jeremy Ben-Ami had witnessed—was nothing in terms of absurdity when you realized that besides the conflict playing out in real life, it was also playing out online.

I knew that I had to investigate.

I had never tried Second Life, and had already written it off as just another manifestation of breathless dot-com hype. I thought it was primarily used by unhappy married people to have virtual affairs with other unhappy married people across the country and end up as the bizarre story at the end of the evening news.

I was right about that. But it was used for other things too, apparently.

Second Life is a virtual environment, accessible from your home computer, where you create a character to represent you and set about giving that character a full virtual life. You buy them clothes, make friends, buy land, build houses, attend parties, date, get married, go to lectures and concerts, engage in political causes, and do pretty much anything else—including, yes, have virtual sex and possibly end up on the real-life evening news.

The politicians running for office all had "campaign offices" in Second Life, and many major corporations had presences as well. Reuters even had a Second Life news bureau. Just recently, the first Second Life millionaire had arisen. This wasn't someone who had made a million "Linden dollars"—the virtual currency used in Second Life—but someone who had made a million real dollars, money she could remove from the virtual world. And she had done it by selling Second Life real estate. Virtual real estate.

And as in everything else, the Middle East and all its troubles had found its way into this virtual world. There was a virtual Israel, virtual Arab neighborhoods, and even virtual Middle East terrorism.

I told Abby all this and said I was going to start playing Second Life as the next stage in my effort to make Middle East peace.

"That sounds stupid," she said. But I was determined. My peacemaking efforts in real life weren't bearing much fruit yet, so maybe the virtual world was my only hope.

So I logged on and created a character who I thought looked vaguely like me. Then I started walking around the virtual world.

For the first few minutes, I didn't find very much. Just green grassy fields, and something that looked like an old, broken wagon. Where was all the action I had heard about? Where were the chainstores, the millionaires, and the virtual pickup bars? Where were the other people? Supposedly there were millions of "residents" of Second Life, but I couldn't find any of them.

Just when I was about to give up on this whole venture, I discovered that instead of just randomly strolling around looking at virtual fields and virtual broken wagons—how, I wondered, did a virtual broken wagon even come to be?—there was a way for me to teleport myself to other locations.

I tried it and discovered a listing of events that were happening at that moment. I picked one of the events randomly, not sure what it was, and clicked on it. A moment later my avatar was being transported to somewhere else in the Second Life universe. And I appeared in front of a woman in a nurse's uniform having sex with a dragon wearing a top hat.

Well, this is awkward, I thought, knowing that somewhere out there in the real world there were two people controlling these two avatars. I had never experienced awkwardness online before, but there was no mistaking it.

Eventually I managed to find the places in Second Life where the Middle East situation really was manifesting. I found the virtual Israel, and I spent some time walking my virtual self through it. Along the way, I saw online versions of many Israeli landmarks, such as the most famous skyscraper in Tel Aviv. There was even an online version of the Western Wall, and right beside it I encountered an online version of some members of Chabad Lubavitch, a messianic and evangelizing sect of Judaism. As in real life, I avoided them. But besides them, I didn't see much street life in the streets of virtual Israel.

After a while, I found my way into a café in what was known as "the Jewish neighborhood of Second Life." Surely, I thought, I would find people there who might be able to tell me about how the conflict played out in their virtual world.

"Abby," I called out from my office. "I found the Jewish neighborhood of Second Life, and I'm going into a café there."

"You're an idiot," she called back cheerily, going about her business in the other room.

I pressed on. And inside the café, I did indeed find some life.

There were about half a dozen characters sitting around the café, drinking virtual coffees, and I went over and sat down at a table near a couple of them. And soon, as weird as it was, I was having a conversation with them about what they called "the Jewish community of Second Life" and the Middle East question.

At the café, I asked some of the other patrons about Israeli-Palestinian issues in Second Life, and they were quick to confirm what I had been told. The conflict played out in Second Life in a big way. There had been several "terrorist attacks" at the virtual Western Wall, they said, and the guy who ran the Wall was thinking of shutting it down.

The terrorist attacks, they explained, consisted of electronic sabotage and vandalism, whereby the Wall and the area around it was defaced with anti-Semitic graffiti, including swastikas that could not be easily removed. But they also told me that they had heard that a jihadi group operating in Second Life had actually killed people—that is, people's *avatars*—and there was concern that something like that could target virtual Israel.

"There's a lot of anti-Semitism in Second Life," one of them told me.

In fact, they said, at times when the *real* Middle East was particularly turbulent, the hostility would spill over directly into Second Life. If there was a raid on Gaza, for example, Second Life Israel would be overwhelmed by virtual protesters, who would make it difficult or impossible for its regular visitors to go about their virtual lives. There would be hurled insults and racist comments, and the usual back-and-forth about occupation, terrorism, and historical rights.

"These Palestinian people show up in Second Life Israel," one of them continued, "and they harass me for 'stealing' their land and occupying Palestine and all that. But it doesn't make any sense. I've never even been to the real Israel. In RL, I live in Pittsburgh. I'm not occupying anything."

"RL," I had learned by this point, meant "real life," as opposed to Second Life, but I wasn't expecting the first guy's invocation of the outside world to earn him a rebuke from one of the other people in the café.

"Hey!" she said, or, rather, typed. "No talking about RL identities."

"It's a major faux pas," a third avatar explained to me, since I had told them all that I was new to all this.

A Second Life faux pas, I thought. You were allowed to disguise your identity as a horse wearing a ballet outfit, but it was apparently socially unacceptable to discuss real life. I was about to throw my hands up with all this and leave the virtual café, when one of these coffee-shop jockeys said something that caught my interest.

"They've even established a Jewish militia in Second Life," he said, "to protect us."

"Actually," one of the coffee-shop guys said, "if you go out to that synagogue out there, you'll find them patrolling."

Now this was getting really bizarre. But obviously, I had to investigate further. So, with some good-byes to my new virtual friends in the virtual coffee shop, I steered my online self outside.

"I'm trying to find a Jewish militia's virtual patrol," I called out to Abby.

"I Should Believe That You Don't Surprising"

The virtual Israel these people had constructed was remarkably developed, especially since I still didn't really understand what the point in all this was. There were celebrations and meetings, virtual religious services, communal areas like the one I was in, and even a fully functioning newspaper for the Jewish "residents" of Second Life called *2-Life*.

Later on, when I left the world of Second Life, I went to the website for that newspaper and paged through some of its issues; I found that it was a fairly sophisticated publication. Someone was putting a lot of time into it. Published several times a year, it gave a rundown of the issues and events facing the Jews of Second Life. These included new developments and projects in their online community, and threats, including a group of Second Life neo-Nazis.

Second Life neo-Nazis. Virtual extremist groups. Online patrols. I wondered what my friends—who spent their days doing normal things like going to work—would think about how I was spending my time. It was like I had entered an alternate bizarre universe, I thought, and then remembered that I pretty much had.

I walked a little distance away from the coffee shop and soon found the synagogue I'd been sent to. I walked through the empty synagogue, marveling at how much detail had been put into its design, and came out the other side, where I saw an avatar coming toward me. A man with a Star of David on his shirt.

"Hello," he said.

I greeted him and asked him if he was with the Jewish militia.
"Who wants to know?" he asked.

I told him that I was looking into how the conflict manifested
"inworld"—a word I had learned from my coffee-shop buddies—
and he proceeded to explain that he was indeed patrolling.

"For what?" I asked. "Or who?"

"For Palestinian terrorists or Nazis," he said.

"So you're just sitting at home," I typed in, "and patrolling
around online for Palestinian terrorists or Nazis?"

His response: "No talking about RL."

Right, I thought, *a faux pas.*

I asked him if I could accompany him on his "patrol," and
he agreed. To my surprise, though, we didn't just stay in Second
Life Israel but instead ventured to areas that were decidedly not
Israeli. Some kind of Palestinian area. A virtual Arab street mar-
ket. A virtual Morocco.

And all the while, we paraded around, with this guy strutting
around with his Star of David shirt. Clearly hoping for some virtual trouble.

We never found any virtual trouble, and I eventually abandoned
that virtual militiaman, but when I did some more reading later,
I found that the things those guys in the Jewish coffee shop had
told me were true. But there was more too. Rumor had it that
besides political campaigns having operations in Second Life, so
did actual organs of the U.S. government, such as the FBI and
possibly even the CIA. The reason for all this, supposedly, was

that terrorists—real-world terrorists—were suspected to be using Second Life for their own goals.

That sounded ridiculous, but what did I know? They could conceivably have been using it for a number of purposes: communication, training, even transferring money. Anything was possible. After all, I had gone on a patrol for online Palestinian terrorists. I had no idea what else might be out there.

But in any case, by now I had decided that my peacemaking future was not online but back in the real world—where something huge was about to happen.

CHAPTER SEVEN

Give Me a Child
for His First Seven Years

In case you are unaware: Barack Obama was elected president.

I thought this boded well for the chances of Middle East peace, but other people immediately began making jokes at my expense. Especially my friend Luke.

"So," he said, "your project's pretty redundant now, huh?"

And: "Do you think you can make peace before him?"

But since I had a jump on the president, I figured that I still had a shot at making peace first. There was also another new development. Despite the fact that they had suffered a setback when George Soros had pulled his money out of their initiative, Jeremy Ben-Ami, Daniel Levy, and their allies had persevered, gathering other donors and building an organizational structure. And, only a little delayed, they had launched their counter to AIPAC after all. It was called J-Street, because Washington DC's grid lacked a "J Street," and they were seeking to fill the pro-Israel but dovish void in DC politics. It was still completely uncertain if they would succeed, and they had miles to go before they could actually match AIPAC's clout, but with the new liberal president, J-Street definitely seemed a good fit with the political zeitgeist.

Over in the Middle East, meanwhile, there were both muted strains of optimism and growing threads of discontent about the new Obama presidency. The Arab world was generally delighted with the new president, but in some sectors of Israeli society and amid the fiercely pro-Israel set in the U.S., there were concerns about him, and the smear efforts that had run throughout the campaign had morphed into a just-under-the-surface hostility.

Meanwhile, Benjamin Netanyahu became Israel's new prime minister. To me—and I was far from the only one—it felt like Israel was moving in the opposite direction from the United States. While the Obama administration had a conciliatory approach to the Middle East and a generally dovish take on foreign affairs, Netanyahu was determined to offer a hard-line approach. I didn't think this would bear much fruit, as it seemed to be the same intransigence—perhaps even heightened—that had played a role in holding up the peace process for years.

Almost immediately the two leaders began tussling in a way that hadn't been seen between an American president and an Israeli prime minister in quite some time—particularly over the continuing Israeli development of settlements in the West Bank. The Obama administration talked tougher and more openly against the settlements than an American administration had done in a while, and although the Netanyahu government made a few concessions and some symbolic gestures toward curtailing them, it mostly pushed back against the American requests to end their expansion. This led the Palestinian leadership to balk at restarting negotiations in earnest, and put a wrench in Obama's plans for some speedy progress.

The settlements were a hot button issue, but there were also other issues that threatened to blow up and pull the new American administration into the Middle East mess. There was the constant simmering tension along the Israeli-Lebanese border, the Hamas-Israel crossfire, and the chance that at any moment Israel might attack Iran to destroy its nuclear capability, possibly unleashing a full-scale regional war. If there was anyone who could benefit from Middle East peace, it was the new American leadership.

So I decided that I should put my competitive streak aside and let the White House know that I was coming to their aid.

During the presidential campaign, I had twice interviewed a man named Kevin, who was one of Obama's Middle East advisors. Kevin had seemed incredibly down to earth, considering that he was playing an important role at the nexus of a historic candidacy and one of the hottest political issues of all. Now that he had been appointed one of the new president's foreign policy advisors, I thought I would get in contact with him to congratulate him. And, through him, give the administration the head's-up that I was trying to interfere.

I sent Kevin an email briefly explaining what I was up to and making the modest suggestion that Kevin give me some assistance or advice from his perch in the White House. To be honest, I more or less expected to be ignored. After all, no matter how approachable and generous with his time Kevin had been during the campaign, he was now a sitting member of the administration and wouldn't have nearly the latitude or motivation to talk to me that he had had before.

And so, when I didn't get a reply for a few days, I wrote this whole idea off. I might have to go forward, I thought, without the support of the Executive Branch.

But then, astonishingly, I got an email from Kevin.

And it said: "Good luck."

There wasn't much more to it than that. Just a few pleasantries about being sorry he had missed me the last time I had been in DC, and then those two words: "Good luck."

This was the first time I had ever received any personal missive from the White House. So even if this was almost certainly just a polite blow-off email, dashed off absently in order to placate me and get me to leave him alone, I decided to take it seriously.

With email so famously bad at conveying tone, Kevin's "good luck" could have meant several different things. It could have been a simple brush-off, which was fairly likely. It could have been a sarcastic put-down, which was probably pretty likely too. Or it could have been an honest expression of support—because, in the end, we were both trying to make peace.

This was highly unlikely, I knew. It was highly unlikely that he cared at all about my project, let alone had enough confidence in it to sincerely offer me good luck. But this was the interpretation I decided I would cling to. And so for the next few days, I told anyone who would listen that the White House was now backing my efforts to make peace.

"Sure they are," Abby said. "Sure they are."

At the same time, I was conflicted about how to proceed with Kevin. On the one hand, I could just decide to accept his well wishes in the best light possible, and not push for any further contact—contact which would in all likelihood just result in me being ignored or even overtly smacked down. Or, I could take his "good luck" at face value, and push further. Maybe he could give me some help. Or, maybe at the end of all this, *I* could tell *him* my findings. He was my link to the Oval Office, after all, and that's where a peace deal would probably need to be pushed from.

I decided not to respond yet, while I considered my next move. Meanwhile, I would just continue casually dropping vague references to everyone that the White House was "behind me." That struck me as a good plan.

But regardless of what happened with Kevin, I knew I had to ratchet up my efforts and talk to some of the power players who had played serious roles in Middle East diplomacy over the years, and who continued to hold some serious sway.

I went to my desk and wrote out a long list of names, hopeful that although I probably wouldn't be able to connect with all of them, a few would be willing to get together and compare notes.

First the former presidents: I decided not to bother with George W. Bush, since he had just left office and was highly unlikely to grant one of his first post-presidency interviews on this subject to some random person with a crazy-sounding mission. So, that left Clinton, Bush Sr., and Carter.

Next, a few secretaries of state: I put down Kissinger, Albright, Baker, and Rice. Then, some prominent U.S. senators.

Finally, I added some Israeli figures, like a former Mossad officer, a former head of the Mossad, and some Palestinians, like a former negotiator and the current head Palestinian representative to the United States.

I figured I'd start with Bill Clinton. When I had worked in the Israeli prime minister's office, the former president had once come to Israel and I'd briefly interacted with his spokesman, who I hoped might now remember me. But when I dug around for his contact details, I discovered that he had since switched jobs. So I made a more formal request to the Clinton Foundation, and waited for a reply.

I made a similar request to the Carter Center, and the woman I spoke to on the phone there was very welcoming. Carter, I figured, was a real possibility. To many Israelis' dismay—and the frustration of successive American administrations—the former president didn't seem to be able to keep quiet about the Middle East. I had high hopes that I might get some of his time.

In the coming days, though, no reply seemed to be forthcoming from either of the two presidents. But I did manage to get through to a senior aide to George Bush Sr., who though disconcertingly formal—he insisted on calling me "Mr. Levey" no matter how many times I tried to get him to call me "Greg"—was helpful. Over the course of a few days, he and I discussed my proposed dialogue with Bush, and I told him more and more about what I was doing, careful to be honest while at the same time trying not to sound too flippant. The end result of our conversation was not good. I pushed to speak to Bush, stressing that I wouldn't ask anything too problematic, but after we went back and forth a few times, it seemed to me that the aide was suggesting that the former president was wary about interviews on foreign affairs, and perhaps particularly uneasy about the Middle East mine field. At almost eighty-five years old, he said, President Bush no longer had the energy to have discussions about it.

I had heard that on his upcoming eighty-fifth birthday, the former president planned to go skydiving, as he had done on several other landmark birthdays. So, essentially, he had the energy to jump out of planes, but not to discuss the Middle East. That would have seemed odd to me once, but it now made total sense.

With Bush out, and no word yet from Clinton or Carter, I moved on to the secretaries of state. I started with Kissinger, who had played such a huge role in events in the region, but couldn't even find an email address or phone number for his consulting firm in New York. I called up the agency that handled his speaking engagements to see if they would connect me, left a message, and got no response. The chances of me getting advice from the man who had won a Nobel Peace Prize looked bleak.

I had a much easier time getting through to Albright—or, rather, her aides—but they told me that the secretary would not be available for such a conversation. They did, however, thank me for "thinking of her." That was nice of them.

At first I thought things were promising with Condoleezza Rice. I emailed one of her people, and she responded positively—copying several other people on her reply email—but she also asked for some more information on my plans. Again, I tried to walk the line between being disrespectful and being dishonest. And again, Rice's aide responded fairly positively, adding even more respondents to our email chain. This went on for several more rounds, and each time more people were added to the list of recipients. None of the others ever contributed to the discussion, but soon it seemed like an endless list of names was getting the emails. I had no idea who any of them were.

I would suggest some possible questions I might ask Rice, trying to sound respectable, and then they would want some clarification on what exactly my agenda was, and I would worry that my cover of respectability was blown. But then more people would be added to the email chain, and I would be asked for more clarification of what exactly I was trying to do.

And then, finally, dutifully copying all the other people on the list, the original person told me that Condoleezza Rice would not be able to have the discussion with me. I guess, somewhere along the way, I must have said something wrong.

James Baker was more receptive. I corresponded with one of his aides for a while, who discussed my proposed conversation with me, and then told me that the secretary would indeed be able to speak with me. The only problem was that he would not be able to do it, even for just a couple of minutes, for a few months. That would be beyond the time I had for my project.

Things were not going well with the heavy hitters at all.

And when I called senators Joe Lieberman and John McCain—two politicians who had played important roles in formulating U.S. foreign policy—their aides never called me back at all. In

McCain's case, I began to call repeatedly, leaving long and—because I was starting to get frustrated—progressively weirder messages about needing to talk to McCain in order to make Middle East peace. In retrospect, I guess it makes sense that nobody from his office got in touch.

I called the Palestinian Mission to the United States, and asked someone there if I could meet with Dr. Nabil Abuznaid, the head of the Mission. He represented the Palestinian Authority in the United States, was close to some of the current Palestinian leadership, and had once been a senior advisor to Yasser Arafat. The person who answered the phone told me that I needed to fax in a request. I did as they asked and waited for their reply.

I contacted the Israeli Embassy in DC, meanwhile, and didn't even get that far. I left messages, and nobody got back to me at all, even though I had previously visited it as an employee of the Israeli government.

It was all a little disheartening. I hadn't expected all, or even most, of these big shots to be receptive me, but I had sort of expected at least one or two of them to be. That I was getting essentially zero traction with this upper echelon of decision makers was frustrating. Didn't they realize I was trying to make peace?

But, if I was honest with myself, I knew this didn't just present strategic problems for me. It also presented personal ones. I had been at this for some time now, and I wasn't getting anywhere. I didn't want to admit it to Abby or Luke or anyone else yet, but my doubts about my whole project were growing steadily. At the outset, I had thought that even if I didn't actually broker peace, I would at least do something positive, like getting people from opposing sides to have a fruitful dialogue, or even just come to understand the situation better myself. Now I was doubting even that. Maybe I was just wasting my time and acting like an idiot.

Maybe it would have helped a little, I thought, if Wayne, the foul-mouthed Brit, had acted as my sounding board, like he had agreed to. But after I had responded to his last email, confirming that this was indeed about "the Israel thing," I hadn't even heard back from him again. My guess was that he had had second thoughts about being involved with the project at all, and I had decided to give up on him completely.

You'll recall that when I had met him, I had first almost accidentally had lunch with a total stranger named Barry. Now, as things got rough, I found myself wishing that I had dined with Barry after all. He hadn't seemed like the kind of guy who would betray me like this.

After checking my email and finding no replies from anyone yet again, I got up from my desk and stared out the window. Had I accomplished anything? I had certainly met some new people who had given me some new perspectives, but it still felt like my project had so far consisted mostly of false starts. It didn't feel like I was getting any traction at all.

Ideally, at a moment like this, I would have been staring out at some windswept desert vista, or maybe at the troubled city of Jerusalem. But not only was I not in the Middle East, but I lived downtown and didn't really have a view at all. So all I was looking at was the wall of the neighboring building.

Staring at that brick wall, I wondered if maybe I should just quit. If maybe I should just give up on making peace or whatever it was I was trying to do. If I should just resign myself to the idea that the conflict was going to plague us all forever, and to an endless future of crazies emailing me. If maybe I should just tell my publisher that no book was forthcoming after all, and the people of the Middle East that no peace was coming either. I had failed them, and failed myself.

That's when the doorbell rang, and my luck began to change.

Here's what I was planning to do with my PeaceMaker boxer shorts. I had never told Abby that I had ordered them, and I had not told her that I had since corresponded with the PeaceMaker people to complain that they hadn't arrived. And I definitely hadn't told her that I was anxiously awaiting their arrival because they had taken on some kind of totemic importance for me.

What I had been planning to do once they arrived was to discreetly put them on, and then, at just the right moment, casually reveal the fact that I had underwear with PEACEMAKER written on the front. I would parade around the apartment wearing them, or wear them when we went to sleep. She may have somehow beaten the PeaceMaker game itself, but I had the underwear.

What I hadn't anticipated, though, was that Abby would be at home when the boxers were delivered.

When the doorbell rang and I came out of my office, she was there and had already spoken on the intercom to whoever was downstairs.

"It's a delivery guy," she said, "with a package for you."

"Hmm," I said, shrugging as if I had no idea what it might be—but hoping that it was what I thought it was. "I'll go see."

I went downstairs and took the delivery, hoping that when I got upstairs, Abby wasn't waiting, so that I could later tell her that the delivery had been something else. Unfortunately, though, she was there, and watched as I opened the package. Inside were two pairs of boxer shorts.

"You ordered PeaceMaker boxer shorts?" she asked, perhaps a little concerned.

For me, the arrival of the boxer shorts felt important. It signaled hope and possibility. Sure, nobody was returning my phone calls, and I still hadn't accomplished a whole lot, but I had done *something*.

I took them back to my desk and resisted the urge to change into them right then and there. I would wait for the right time.

I checked my email and, as if the boxer shorts had actually turned the tide of my luck, I found an intriguing note from my friend Jacob, a New Yorker who had moved to Israel some years before. When I had been living there, he had been the center of a vibrant community of Anglo expats who had found themselves in Tel Aviv for one reason or another. We had banded together because of the familiarity of language and culture, and most of us had not lasted there very long. But Jacob remained, and had met and married another American ex-pat living in Israel. They even talked about staying there permanently.

Jacob was one of my closest friends, and he knew all about my project. He had previously said that he found it strange that I was trying to make peace from so far away, but even so, he was eager to help. And in his email, he told me that one of the most prominent would-be peacemakers in Israeli history—among many other things an architect of the Oslo Accords, the Israeli-Palestinian peace process in the 1990s—wanted to talk to me.

Yossi Beilin and the faction of Israeli politics that he represented had fallen out of favor in Israel in recent years, but at one point, during the optimistic nineties, he and his compatriots had been ascendant. Beilin had been deeply involved in the process that led to the first tentative steps toward reconciliation, and culminated with the Yitzhak Rabin-Yasser Arafat handshake on the White House lawn. More recently, he had also been the most visible face of the Geneva Initiative—which Daniel Levy, of J-Street, had also been deeply involved with. In Israel, Beilin was often synonymous with the dovish approach to diplomacy.

For many in the Israeli public, though, his name was also synonymous with failure and naïveté. On the Right, and even in the Center, he represented a paradigm of thinking that was thought to have been proven wrong when the Second Intifada had been launched. His plans had been premised on the idea that the Palestinians honestly wanted a fair solution and would then cease their violence. For many in Israel, the Intifada had discredited that notion, and Beilin's continued optimism was seen as obtuseness.

At the same time, many of the ideas he and his allies had first pioneered had wormed their way firmly into mainstream Israeli political discourse. Beilin had been one of the earliest champions of a two-state solution, which was now given at least lip service by almost every Israeli leader, and some even argued that the reason Ariel Sharon had withdrawn from the Gaza Strip was because of the PR-spectacle of the Geneva Initiative—Beilin's fake peacemaking effort.

But why did he want to talk to me? Were my own peacemaking efforts somehow being noticed in the Middle East?

No, I found out from Jacob. They were not. How Jacob had connected with Beilin I never really found out, but the former peacemaker was writing a book about young North American Jews who had visited or engaged with Israel, and the effects it had had on them. And he wanted to interview me for it.

Okay, I told Jacob. I'd do it, but I would have some questions for Beilin as well.

Things were suddenly moving. I had my PeaceMaker underwear, and one of the fathers of the Israeli peace movement was going to call me. It was too late in the day in Israel now for me to expect a phone call from Beilin, but all this had given me confidence to make a decision about what to do with Kevin, my White House contact.

I would call him again and follow up. After all, he *had* wished me good luck.

So I made the call to the White House and got a serious-sounding operator whose tone of voice suggested that I might be calling to report an imminent attack on the homeland. Kevin wasn't there, but she said that she'd be sure to have him call me back.

I hung up and sat back in my chair, a bit more optimistic. The wheels were turning at least a little.

* * *

I hoped that when I heard from Yossi Beilin or Kevin I would be able to move forward in a big way. But in the meantime, I decided to go backward a little—and revisit the place where I had first heard about the Israeli-Palestinian conflict.

That's how I ended up outside my former elementary school later that afternoon, watching the kids play in the schoolyard. I smiled as I saw one of the younger kids licking a dirty brick wall. I had probably once licked that same wall, I thought nostalgically. It had been in this very playground that another child had once whipped around his jacket, catching the zipper on my forehead and slicing it open in a long clean cut. And it had been here that I had once run straight toward a much bigger kid, convinced that he would move out of the way before I reached him, and as a result been knocked unconscious for the first time. Those had been good times.

It had also been here that I had first heard the word "Palestinian" and been educated in Zionist history and philosophy, which is why I had come here today. To see if going back to where it had started for me would help me move forward.

In the Middle East, the way that children were educated was a controversial issue. In Israel, for example, there had long been a debate about how to teach children about the origins of their country. Was it appropriate to tell them about the Palestinians who had been displaced at Israel's founding? Even if one believed that that displacement was a necessary but unfortunate moral imperative, did that mean that children growing up in a complicated place should be weighed down by the burden of that history? In recent years, there had been more of an effort to engage with the less appealing parts of Zionist history, but for most of Israel's existence, the more unsavory bits had generally been ignored or passed over quickly. The displacement of the Palestinians, the bloody actions sanctioned by some of the state's founders to secure a home for the Jewish people, the suffering of Palestinians in Gaza and the West Bank, and the difficulties and injustices often experienced by Arab citizens of Israel had been largely ignored.

Palestinian children had it worse—and weirder. Over the past few years, for example, one of the more popular characters on Hamas TV was a Mickey Mouse lookalike named Farfour, who preached about Islamic supremacy and told children about the glories of martyrdom, recommending that they "annihilate the Jews." There had also been a character named Nahoul the Bee, who, like Farfour, was eventually martyred on the show at the hands of the Jews. More recently, there was a brown bear named Nassur who had come to Palestine to join the holy war, and had reportedly hinted on air that he had come from Iran. He was joined by a giant Jew-eating bunny named Assud.

But even in North America, the issue of how children, especially Jewish and Arab children, learned about the conflict was interesting and important. And this school, between getting my head cut open and stupidly running into bigger children, was where I myself had first gotten inklings of it.

It had been eighteen years since I had graduated from eighth grade, but as I sat in the car outside, watching today's version of who I had been play in the schoolyard, the memories came flooding back.

It was a Zionist Jewish school. Each morning we had sung the Israeli national anthem, and on special days we had been made to dress up in blue and white, the colors of the Israeli flag. Our Hebrew and Jewish studies teachers had been Israeli women who, it had always seemed to me, had been kicked out of the Israeli army for excessive brutality and sent directly to our school. At the time, I was pretty sure that the most infamous one—with the appropriate name, Witchler—had probably been personally responsible for the vast majority of violence in the Middle East.

And when our graduation had been approaching, it had been Witchler—whom I remember as being eight feet tall and carrying a police baton at all times—who had taken charge of our ceremony. Instead of it being a dignified or celebratory event, though, she and some of her colleagues had other ideas. Our graduation would be a musical in which we pretended to be various ethnic stereotypes and danced around in vaguely offensive costumes while singing songs with mildly racist undertones. My impression of a graduation, even an eighth-grade graduation, involved caps and gowns, and maybe some marching. In our graduation, though, we were being divided into groups representing the various Jewish factions from around the world that had immigrated to Israel. Instead of wearing caps and gowns, we had to dress up as Yemenites, Ethiopians, Russians, and assorted other nationalities.

"Why are they doing this to us?" I remember my friend David asking me. "I just want to get my diploma and go to high school next year."

"I don't know why they are doing this," I told David. "I think they just hate us."

As graduation approached, instead of going out to the playground at recess, we would be summoned to a practice.

"To the multipurpose room!" Witchler would shriek at us. "Now! Now!"

And as if we were being conscripted into a war we didn't believe in, we marched off sullenly. There, in the multipurpose room—whose only purpose I could ever discern was as a place to make us do humiliating things—we divided into our assigned ethnic groupings and rehearsed. The groups each had a moment in the spotlight, singing songs about their respective countries and doing what our Israeli teachers imagined were native dances.

At one point in the performance, I remember, everything stopped for a moment so that a kid named Philip could say his one line.

He would step forward proudly and, apropos nothing, proclaim, "Tunis is the best!"

And then the different groups would begin dancing again, or singing about their particular cuisine. Or whatever inanity they had been engaged in before Philip's big line.

But while nobody was happy about the graduation situation, I felt especially bad for a boy named Steven Gold, whose life Witchler was making particularly hellish. Steven had somehow unwittingly displayed some aptitude at singing that the rest of the boys lacked—with all of us going through puberty, I'm not sure what they expected from our adolescent voices—and he wasn't happy about it.

"You'll be our star," Witchler had said, and not in a way that left any room for a decision on his part.

"I don't want to be the star," he told me later, and I nodded sympathetically. Of course he didn't. None of us would have wanted to. As far as I could tell, in fact, none of us even wanted to be up on that stage at all, let alone "starring" in this bizarre production.

In our preparations, meanwhile, there were strange songs about the foods of Tunisia and the dances of South America, and the implicit threat that if we didn't cooperate in this circus, we might not graduate and would have to do the same thing the following year. Also, it was stressed to us that our graduation ceremony was in part about us, but in larger part about the "ingathering of exiles" in Israel—the different nationalities we were all role-playing on stage. Even as we prepared to leave the school behind, we were told, we were doing our bit for the Zionist cause.

I can't actually remember which group I was assigned to— though I seem to have a vague memory of having to dress up as if I were from Yemen—because I was the one kid in the school who was actually kicked out of the graduation ceremony. I refused to sing the songs and just mouthed them instead, and when Witchler noticed this, I was punished by being banished from the part of the performance where we were assigned to ethnic groups.

Even to this day, that was one of the happiest moments of my life. I was thrilled that I wouldn't have to be onstage with the rest of my classmates as they were forced through a public humiliation that was sure to leave psychological scars on everyone involved. In fact, I remember a few of them being envious of me, not because they felt any misgivings about the odd ethnic stereotyping—we were all a little young for that—but because even besides that, the whole thing felt more than a little off.

When I later compared notes with a friend who attended a nearby public school, I was jealous to learn that his graduation ceremony had had no embarrassing songs and dances and no bizarre multicultural show tunes. It was pretty much just shaking hands and being congratulated for finishing eighth grade. Maybe with caps and gowns, but definitely not with folk dancing and ethnic stereotypes.

So now, all these years later, looking at the kids playing in the schoolyard, I wondered if their graduation ceremonies would be like mine was. Would that kid licking the wall have to dress as an Ethiopian tribesman and sing songs about escaping to Israel? And more to the point, what were they learning about the Middle East? It wasn't as if I expected it to be any more nuanced than what my classmates and I had learned—after all, the oldest among them was just thirteen years old—but I wondered if the curriculum had developed at all. In the time since I had left the school, so much had changed. There was far more recognition about the need for a Palestinian state, but there had also been so much blood spilled in failing to reach that goal. We had learned about the conflict in stark, easily understood terms of good and evil. Were these kids learning about it with any more complexity?

Hold on, I thought, *is that teacher looking at me?*

Indeed, a teacher in the schoolyard was staring at me, with an odd look on her face. I didn't recognize her, but I wondered if it was possible that she recognized me. Could it be that she remembered me as the kid who had been kicked out of graduation for refusing to sing songs about the beauty of Yemen? More likely, I decided, was that she just found it suspicious that a strange man was just outside the school gates, staring at the children. It was lucky, I thought, that she didn't know how delighted I had been earlier about the arrival of my "special underwear."

I smiled at her and nodded. It was time to leave.

But how much nuance can you expect a child's education to have? Is it possible to try to teach kids to see the complexity in the situation and avoid one-sided thinking? As I headed away from my old school, I didn't know. But I did know that I'd once seen a school try to do just that.

When I'd been working at the UN, one of my side duties had been to give little lectures to visiting groups of high school and college students about the Israeli perspective on world affairs. One of these groups had been particularly interesting, not only because they were from a Muslim high school, but because of the reason they had requested to meet with someone from the Israeli delegation. The national Model UN was coming up, and they were going to be playing Israel.

It was a bit disorienting when the group filed into the conference room. They were mostly of South Asian descent, with a smattering of Arab faces among them, and most of the girls wore hijabs. But they immediately started asking questions about how they should best state Israel's case at the Model UN.

The kids were from a Muslim high school in Queens, and their teacher—a religious Muslim herself—had told me that she had specifically requested that her students be assigned to play the Israeli delegation.

"They are exposed to one side of the political debate about Israel," she told me, "and I felt it was important for them to really understand the other side."

My discussion with them was fascinating.

"As Israel," one of the girls wearing a head scarf asked me, "how can we convince the others that all we're trying to do is protect our citizens from terrorism?"

She asked the question earnestly, and she looked completely serious, but I couldn't help myself from smiling because of how incongruous this was—the image of a religious Muslim wholeheartedly taking the Israeli position. Even so, I answered the question as best as I could, and the student who had asked it took diligent notes, and then her classmates proceeded to pepper me with a long list of similar questions about diplomatic strategy from the Israeli position.

It was clear that these were good students and good kids. Their questions were astute, and they had done their reading. There was no question that they knew more about Israel and its people than I had when I had been in high school. And after a while, I began to forget that they were religious Muslims and that Israel's well-being was probably not of paramount importance to them.

When our meeting was over, they told me that the Model UN was soon and would be held at the actual UN building in New York, using the real UN chambers and conference halls. They, the

"Israeli" delegation, would be sitting in the real Israeli delegation's seats and trying to accomplish the same goals the actual Israelis struggled with each day.

I had to see it.

So, with the teacher and the kids' permission, on a Saturday not long after that, I showed up at the UN to find it transformed into a surreal, younger version of itself. At the time I was used to frequenting the building's corridors and working amid the hundreds of adult diplomats, which made it especially odd to see the metamorphosis it had undergone. Teenagers in suits walked around in small groups, talking in hushed tones and carrying folders and stacks of documents. As they walked by, I heard words like "Security Council," "veto power," and "General Assembly." If not for the occasional pierced eyebrow and the lack of gray hair, I could easily have thought that it was just another workday at the UN.

When I found my group, they were having a discussion about a draft resolution that they were about to introduce for voting. In hushed discussions, they strategized about who their likely allies were, and who they needed to lobby. Apparently this didn't go well, because later I saw one of the girls in the discussion come storming out of a UN chamber. She was a sixteen-year-old named Osia, who wore full Muslim religious attire.

"Why does everyone hate us?" she asked the rest of the group.

Later, over coffee in a UN café, the school's Pakistani principle told me that some of the kids' parents were not happy with this experiment.

"They did not want their children to defend Israel's actions," he said. "I had to speak with them and try to convince them. They wanted us to switch countries. Some of them are still not at all happy that their children are involved in this."

So when I encountered Osia again, I asked her about this generational issue.

"At family gatherings," she said, "you always hear about the conflict, about the way that Israel uses advanced military equipment and the Palestinians just use stones. But now I understand a little more. It is surrounded by hostile nations, so now I see Israel's military necessity."

After one session, where the "Palestinian" delegation—who all had thick Mexican accents—had been particularly hostile, one of Osia's young Bangladeshi classmates declared, "We in Israel have to be good at self-defense, ready to defend ourselves at any time."

She realized I was listening and paused, clearly recognizing how odd this sounded coming from her.

"By assuming another viewpoint, you make a stranger out of yourself," she told me. "But at this moment, I am an Israeli."

Over the course of the day, as these little delegates shuffled in and out of meetings in the actual UN chambers, I continued to try to probe a little more into what they really thought. One of them told me that she had been feuding with her father as a result of this project, and that he had been one of the parents who had tried to stop it.

"He is very angry that I am doing this," she told me, "because Israel kills Muslims."

And, after a few more attempts, I was able to get some more out of Osia too.

"Jews have a right to a country," she told me, "but why does it have to be in Palestine? Why do they have to be intruders?"

"Do you have any Jewish friends?" I asked her and one of her friends, and they both shook their heads.

"Honestly," Osia told me, "I think you are the first one I have ever really met."

Then she went to retake her seat as the Israeli delegate at the General Assembly.

But if all this was surreal, the final results of the Model UN were a lot more grounded in reality. I sat with the Israeli delegation as the results were announced by the judges. Across dozens of categories, they scored no wins at all. Perhaps they had not deserved any, I thought, or perhaps they had just been robbed, like Israel so often was at the real UN. Whatever the case, this caused the kids to drop their diplomatic facades. After the weeks of preparation they had gone through for this day, the kids looked heartbroken. A few of them even burst into tears.

"Why was Israel treated so badly?" one of them asked as the event came to a close.

On my way home from my old Hebrew school, I passed the little fruit stand and looked in. My grocer wasn't there—another man was filling in for him—and I walked on, disappointed. With memories of both my time at Hebrew school and of my time spent with those Muslim kids at the UN, I was in a sort of spacey, unfocused mood.

But when I got back to my desk and checked my email, there was an important reminder of the progress I had been making earlier in the day. Kevin from the White House had emailed me. His "good luck" email had apparently not just been a brush-off.

Yes, he said. We needed to talk.

CHAPTER EIGHT

I Am Not Proud of My Behavior

I called Kevin at the White House the next morning, and again a secretary told me that he wasn't there but he would call me back. There wasn't much time to dwell on this, though, because as I sat wondering if I had pushed my luck with him, my cell phone rang. It was Yossi Beilin calling from Israel.

At the outset of our conversation, I told him that I would be happy to answer the questions he had for me for his book, but in return I wanted to ask him some questions of my own. He sounded amused by this, and agreed.

His questions were about my experience in Israel, about how I had ended up visiting and then moving there, and briefly working for the Israeli government. He also asked me about how the experience had affected my relationship with the Jewish state and my feelings toward the Middle East.

"It's complicated," I told him.

"I'll have to read your book," he said.

"I can send a copy to you."

"No, no," he said, "I'll buy one."

I definitely liked this guy.

So, even though it *was* complicated, I proceeded to give Beilin some of my thoughts about the region and my relationship to it: some of the stuff that was in my first book, and some of the stuff that I had thought about more recently as I tried to solve the conflict myself. He seemed genuinely interested in my experiences, asking probing questions focusing more on how I saw my relationship with Israel than on substantive political issues.

And then we switched roles, and it was my turn to ask questions.

I told him that in my own efforts, I was sometimes facing moments of doubt. Doubt that I was getting any closer to peace. Doubt that I could persevere.

"What pushes you forward against the odds?" I asked him.

"I fought in four wars," he said. "Isn't that enough? The greatest push for me came in the 1973 war. Before that, I was mainstream to the left, but mainstream for sure. The war in 1973 changed my life. We'd had six years of hubris. In order to have security, people believed we needed more territory. But in 1973, the Golan Heights settlements became an impediment instead. It was more difficult to take kids living there and hide them than to defend an empty area. The settlements didn't secure Tel Aviv. They didn't defend us."

I was aware that in 1973, six years after Israel had taken over the West Bank, Gaza, and the Golan Heights and first began to populate them with its own citizens, it had been the victim of a surprise attack by Egypt and Syria. This was probably the closest Israel has ever come to being destroyed; it also resulted in the downfall of a government and still remains a particularly bitter memory in the Israeli consciousness. Although they are now gone from Gaza, the population of Israelis living in the always contentious West Bank and the only occasionally controversial Golan Heights has, of course, only skyrocketed in the decades since the war.

I noted that nowadays the Israeli government and public seemed to be moving rightward, and I asked, "Are you hopeful?"

"I am hopeful," he said, "because people are now talking in my language. Even people in the Likud. If you want to keep Israel Jewish and democratic, you have to have a Palestinian state."

"Do Israelis and Palestinians need the U.S. in order to make peace?" I asked.

The more I had thought about it, the more this seemed to be a key question that divided people on how to make peace. Should the United States get fully involved or not? One side, generally the more aggressively pro-Israel side, wanted the United States to maintain its hands-off approach and let Israel determine its own security needs and decide its own destiny. The other side, generally more eager to push forward to a sustainable solution, wanted the United States to use its influence to push both Israelis and Palestinians to make the concessions seen as needed for such an end goal.

For Beilin, the answer was clear. He considered his words for a moment, and then answered carefully.

"When the Palestinians are too weak, and the Israelis are too reluctant, then we need the Americans," he said. "And that's the case today."

The power imbalance between Israelis and Palestinians, he felt, prevented the Palestinians from being able to unilaterally move toward a solution, while the Israelis were hamstrung by internal politics and extremist strands within their populace. Only if the United States were to flex its muscles, making incentives for the parties to take action, could there be progress.

I had one more question, of course.

"How can I personally make peace?" I asked. "Preferably without leaving home much."

I was never sure how people would handle this question, and while I waited for Beilin to answer, I hoped I hadn't somehow offended him. But when he responded, he seemed to take my question quite seriously.

"First of all, it is very difficult to make peace from your parlor," he said. "There is no question about it."

Well, at least it's not just me, I thought, and then considered his use of the word "parlor." His English was really good, and this was one of the very few awkward phrases he had used. But, honestly, I liked his wording better than my own.

Beilin paused again, carefully deciding what advice to give me for my quest. Meanwhile, I had the image of Abby coming home to find me wearing my PeaceMaker boxer shorts and surveying our apartment.

"Welcome to my parlor," I would say proudly.

And then she would file for divorce.

"Look," Beilin continued, snapping me out of this, "you need to convey the message that American Jewry is a very liberal group that believes that Middle East peace is important. That's not necessarily the belief on Capitol Hill. That's why liberal groups like J-Street are important. They're not anti-Israel Jews, but pro-Israel Jews who believe in peace. Being pro-peace is being pro-Israel. An impediment is the belief in the U.S. government that Jews don't want peace. That may be the case in the establishment, but not in the rank and file. Show them that."

Okay, I thought. *I will.*

But first I wanted to speak with the grocer. It had been a while since I had conversed with him, and I wondered if my recent experiences and conversations might help me to further break the ice. Perhaps he had some thoughts on AIPAC or Jeremy Ben-Ami, or on Yossi Beilin.

So I marched down to the grocery store, hoping he would be there this time, unsure if he would even remember me, and not certain on how I planned to proceed. Maybe, I thought, he would be playing Arabic music again, providing me a bridge to conversation.

I found him outside the little stand, smoking a cigarette and watching the passersby. I smiled at him and approached, and he looked at me and nodded, without a smile. His expression seemed to say, "This idiot again. The one who used a pineapple to try to hit on me."

But I was determined to change his impression of me. And so I went into the little kiosk and, after another couple of moments, the grocer put out his cigarette and followed. Instead of Arabic music, he had the radio on, which was playing a local news report.

He looked at me. I looked at him.

Then I looked at some broccoli.

I was pretty sure he remembered me—the grocer, not the broccoli—and so I decided to just jump into conversation.

"How are you?" I asked.

"Fine," he said, and didn't add anything further.

It was interesting, I thought, that I was spending so much time with people who wouldn't shut up about the Middle East, but was having so much trouble getting into a conversation about it with this guy. It also occurred to me that because of the circles I was running in these days, I was starting to forget how touchy a subject the Middle East was—how full of land mines it was and how most normal people avoided the subject whenever they could.

And here I was specifically trying to bring it up. With a Palestinian. With someone who, at least by the compass of ethnicity, was on the opposing side of the conflict.

But should it really have been such a touchy issue? Neither of us lived there. Neither of us would die in the endemic violence there. Did the weight of history—in his case, personal history—mean that we couldn't just discuss it rationally? Would I necessarily offend him? Would we necessarily hate each other?

A commercial was playing on the radio now. An excited voice proclaimed that because the economy had fallen apart and housing prices were so low, they were offering a deal whereby you could buy a house in Florida and a house in the Northeast for one low price.

"Forget about winter," the excited voice said, "with your own place in the sun."

It felt fitting that they were talking about real estate, about housing, when this whole Middle East thing really boiled down to the same thing. It was about ownership, about domesticity—about a sense of home. In North America, there was lots to be had if you had the money. In the Middle East, it demanded a higher premium.

I noticed suddenly that the grocer was looking at me funny, and I wondered if he was thinking the same thing.

Then I realized that I had been standing there quietly for a while, listening to the radio. And I noticed that one of my hands had somehow drifted to an avocado and was resting on it lazily.

But then something interesting happened. The commercial ended and the news came on again, this time talking about international news. Specifically, the Middle East.

"A new spate of violence in the Middle East," the news reporter said.

I considered this, and wondered if it could even be thought of as news. Violence in the region was so expected and constant that he might as well have reported on "the strong possibility of there being weather today," or said, "This just in: our researchers have determined that you are listening to the radio."

But, obviously, this gave me a great bridge to political conversation with the grocer, and I pondered how to best proceed.

"Hey," I might say, "you're from the Middle East. What do you think of the new spate of violence? How does it compare to the old spates of violence? They don't make spates like that anymore, huh? Huh?"

"The Middle East," I said lamely, pointing upward to indicate the radio report, even though the radio was clearly not up at all, but behind the cash register.

Then I just stopped, as if that sentence fragment said it all.

He shook his head, and I was unsure if he was indicating his disapproval of the violence in the Middle East or of me. By this point he was probably equally sick of both. But it turned out he was actually talking about the Middle East.

"It never stops," he said, shaking his head. "Terrible."

Finally the two of us were in business.

"Why do you think it never stops?" I asked.

"Because they're all crazy," he said. "All crazy. All of them."

It was time to finally come clean.

"You know," I told him, "the reason I came here is to ask you about the Middle East."

He looked at me with an expression that was part suspicion and part confusion, which I knew I deserved. And for the next minute or so, I quickly explained to him what I was doing—my quest, my book, and all the different people I was talking to for my project.

He nodded for a moment before speaking. I didn't know what he was going to say, but when he answered, it wasn't what I expected.

"So you don't want to buy that avocado?" he asked.

And with that I realized that at some point I had picked up the avocado that my hand had previously just been lightly touching, and I was now cupping it in front of me. I looked down at it and saw that it was slightly grayer than an avocado should be and that it felt wholly overripe.

"No, I want to buy it," I said, aware that would mean coming home with yet more inedible produce.

"Good." The grocer nodded.

Empowered by this, I pushed on.

"So," I asked, "do you think the Middle East situation will ever be solved?"

"Nah. Nah, never."

"Why not?"

"They just want to fight," he said.

"Who?"

"All of them."

I continued pressing him and eventually got a handle on his basic take on the situation. He definitely had a harsher view of Israel and Israelis than I did—"they're all trained murderers," he said, and leveled the majority of blame on them—but he cast his fellow Palestinians in a pretty negative light as well. He said that if they stopped their violence, then he thought that Israel would no longer have what he called "the excuse" to occupy Palestinian land and keep the Palestinians under its thumb. They were led into this counterproductive violence, he said, by desperation because of Israeli actions and by their religious leaders, who were more interested in maintaining their own power and privilege than in helping their people. And, he added, the trouble could also be blamed on the other Arab countries who "even preferred the Jews to them."

"It's a big catastrophe," he told me, "full of people who just want to make it even worse every day."

"And you think there are people to blame on both sides?" I asked.

He nodded, then asked, "Do you know who Sharon was?"

Yes, I told him. I did.

"Sharon started this," he said. "Sharon. And Hamas made it worse. Sharon and Hamas."

"So what should I do?" I asked.

He squinted his eyes at me, confused. Clearly, he had really not taken it in when I told him what I was trying to do.

"What would you do?" I asked. "What's *your* plan?"

"My plan?" he said, pausing. "Well, I'm thinking of going out to work for the highway companies out West. You know, with all the development going on, there's a lot of jobs out there."

I wanted to tell him that he shouldn't go off to work for the "highway companies," whatever that even meant. I wanted to say that he should stay at the produce stand, and that maybe together we could put an end to the Middle East conflict. We were just getting started.

But I didn't have time to say any of that, because just then, on the street outside, I saw someone I knew.

I told the grocer I would be back for the avocado, and raced out to catch up with him. His name was Amir—and he was Israeli.

Here's the story about Amir. And: I'm not especially proud of my initial behavior.

At a party Luke had thrown a few months before at some downtown hipster bar, I met Amir. He was my age, and had recently arrived from Israel for a job. At some point in the past,

Luke, whom Amir now worked with, had told him about my own connections with Israel, and Amir wanted to know a little more.

We were in a loud, dark bar, surrounded by people with skinny ties and T-shirts with aggressively ironic references to 1980s pop culture. People who drank Pabst Blue Ribbon while discussing the relative merits of indie rock bands so obscure that even some of the musicians in the bands hadn't heard of them. And it was there that Amir and I discussed my experiences with Middle East politics and his impressions of the forces at work in his homeland.

Now here's the part I'm not proud of. Toward the end of our conversation, Amir said that one stark difference he noticed between Israel and North America was that in his opinion, people in Israel were more sincere. In particular, he said, he was referring to the way he felt people in North America had said welcoming things to him upon his arrival on this side of the world, promising that they would help him get settled, take him out, and act as a support grid for him. Then they just receded and didn't provide any real help. That would not happen in Israel, he told me, where people meant what they said.

I had heard this complaint many times before from Israelis living abroad and, to be perfectly honest, it had always irritated me. Not only had I not found the Israelis in Israel particularly helpful to newcomers—an Israeli cab driver had once dropped me off on the side of the road because I hadn't understood a joke he had been trying to tell me—but I didn't think those of us from our side of the world were more unwelcoming than we ought to be. It was true that we didn't overwhelm newcomers with immediate warmth, but I'd spent time in a lot of other countries—including, of course, Israel—and I didn't think we were any worse than anyone else. And certainly not worse than Israelis, who sometimes actually bragged about their national level of rudeness.

And so that's why I made the decision I did. The decision I am not proud of.

I would be warm and welcoming to this newcomer beyond anything that was expected—or anything that was appropriate. I would be nice to him to the point where he would begin to resent me. I would call him all the time to check on how his day had been, and show up at his door with soup if he was sick. I would invite him to awkward dinners at romantic restaurants with Abby and me, without warning her ahead of time, and I would insist that he come with me to any family event I had, even if it was out of town. Sure, I didn't know him at all, and was busy trying to make Middle East peace, but if he *thought* only Israelis were able to be good hosts, then he had another "think" coming.

I looked over and saw that Abby, who was chatting with a friend of Luke's, was watching me out of the corner of her eye, no doubt wondering why I was spending so much time talking to this stranger, and what that weird half smile on my face was about.

"You're just being a jerk," she said to me on the way home, after I told her about my plan. "And you're doing exactly what he says we do. Being insincere. Promising to help and then not doing it."

"But I *am* going to do it," I said, proceeding to tell her about the phone calls, the soup, the family gatherings and, despite my initial intentions, the romantic dinners.

She just nodded, taking it all in stride, and only flinching a bit at the part about the romantic dinners.

"Eventually, though," she said, "you're going to stop doing it and—"

"No," I cut in, "I will never stop. I will continue bombarding him with kindness until he begs me to leave him alone."

"You're being a jerk," she said again.

But Amir didn't think I was a jerk when I text messaged him the next day to tell him that it had been nice to meet him. (Yes, I had asked for his phone number, which had only been a little weird.) And he didn't think I was a jerk when I called him the day after that to invite him out with some friends of mine, or when I requested him as a friend on Facebook the morning after that.

But here's the thing. As I started hanging out with Amir, I began to legitimately like him a lot, and I started to feel bad about the whole plan. Pretty soon, we'd actually become real friends, and I began to worry that he'd find out the reason I'd initially started spending time with him was just to prove a point.

Maybe, I thought, *I was being a jerk after all.*

But I was hopeful that he might never find out. And there was no reason he had to, unless I wrote it down in a book or something.

Amir had grown up in southern Israel, and his family still lived there, in relatively close proximity to the missiles that were flung over the fence by Palestinians in Gaza. As a kid, he had been an active member of the Labor youth movement, which was connected to the center left Labor Party that had dominated Israeli political life for the first half of the state's existence. Although the party continued to play an important role in government, in recent years it had been repeatedly trounced in the polls and rel-egated to junior member status in various coalition governments. No more did its liberal, dovish approach to governing play a seri-ous role in Israel's halls of power. Right-wing hawks had over-taken it in popularity among the Israeli people.

"The country has changed a lot," Amir said to me once. "It scares me what is happening there."

Amir was by no means a far Leftist. His views were pretty firmly those of his Labor Party, which was reasonably close to the Center on the spectrum of possibility. It was a social-democratic party, which though never outright hawkish was willing to sup-port the use of force when necessary. The present-day version of the party had been compared to Bill Clinton's Democrats or Tony Blair's Labor Party.

Amir told me he was proud to be an Israeli, and he had duti-fully served in the army. There, his job had been in the military's central headquarters in Tel Aviv, doing something he couldn't tell me about because it was "secret," but which he also assured me was "totally uninteresting."

But he said that he saw Israel swinging further to the Right, both on foreign affairs and in its treatment of minorities within its own borders, and he didn't like it. He also didn't seem to really like how the conflict manifested over here.

"Let me ask you a question," he once said to me, when we were riding the subway together—he was going to an Elton John–Billy Joel concert, and I had run into him on the subway platform. "Why do so many people here care about the Middle East? I mean, why does it matter to you all so much?"

I told him I didn't know. And, of course, this was one of the main questions spurring my own project.

"Because I'm Israeli," he said, "Jewish people are always inviting me to some rally or fund-raiser for Israel. I look at the flyers and try to figure out where the money is going, and a lot of the time I can't figure it out. So, let me ask you, where is it going?"

I shrugged and told him I didn't know. It was probably different on a case-by-case basis. As far as I understood it, some of that money, depending on the organization behind the particular event, did indeed go to helping regular Israelis struggling through the difficulties of daily life in a war zone. But, I told him, I also knew that sometimes the money went for the expansion of settlements, or to Israeli politicians not amenable to peace.

Amir nodded, scowling.

So when I ran out from the fruit stand to intercept Amir on the street, I wondered briefly if maybe it was an opportunity for an impromptu summit. I could just pull Amir into the fruit stand and introduce him to the grocer, encouraging him to buy some of the stand's "fabulous" produce in order to butter up the grocer. Then, over carrots and pineapples, the three of us would iron out the details of a Middle East peace plan. Both of them seemed pretty conciliatory, so maybe it was possible. Afterward, they would present it to their respective governments. Then there would be a ceremonial signing of a declaration of peace in front of the fruit stand, and the gathered world dignitaries would all share a snack of mediocre fruits and vegetables.

But, instead of all that, Amir had some things he wanted to tell me.

The first: "My father didn't like your book."

"Oh," I said. I wasn't sure how to respond and was amused by his typical Israeli directness. I didn't know his father at all, nor that he had even read my book. "Well, that's too bad."

"I gave it to him because I thought he'd like it," he said, "but he thinks you're a whiner."

I nodded. That was definitely a possibility.

But this was pretty much a dead end as far as conversation went, and so I was glad when he changed the subject to a Dutch girl he had recently gone on a few dates with.

"All she does all day is yell about how evil Israel is," he said, "and how horrible Israelis are."

I was confused. This was someone he had been seeing?

"It's like that's all she cares about," he went on. "Now, I'm obviously not Mr. Right-wing, but it starts to bother me eventually, you know?"

"How did you meet her?" I asked.

"She was outside the supermarket," he said, "yelling stuff about the occupation."

"I see." I nodded. "Then I guess it shouldn't have been a surprise that she was so passionate about the Middle East."

"No, I guess not."

His new love interest had been outside the supermarket, handing out leaflets about what she saw as Israel's crimes and stopping passersby to let them know about them. Amir the Israeli had struck up a conversation, and there had been some attraction, and then some dates. He had since decided that he didn't want a relationship with the firebrand, but was still hanging around with her—and spending most of that time arguing.

"She's a communist," he said, "an actual communist. And all of her friends are too. I've never met people like this before. She's fascinating."

I asked him if maybe I should talk to her for my project.

"I thought you might want to do that," he said. "I'll ask her, and I'm sure she'll say yes. She wants to discuss this stuff all the time."

He paused, then added, "But I have to warn you. Be careful what you tell her. She's a very strange person."

CHAPTER NINE

People with Nothing Better to Do

It was the first time in my life I thought I had come close to caus-ing someone's head to explode just by speaking to them. It wasn't Amir's friend, but someone probably more interesting.

Her name was Samar Assad. She was in her late thirties, and was a former negotiations advisor to the Palestinian Authority and now the executive director of the Palestine Center, a non-profit that worked to disseminate the Palestinian point of view in the United States in order to help guide American policy. The Palestine Center was one of the primary think tanks in the United States devoted to the Palestinian cause, and when I had contacted them to see if one of their people would meet with me to get a Palestinian take on the American relationship to the region, Samar had seemed like the perfect choice.

I had arranged a meeting with her, but had not given her the full scoop on my background. Until now, when I told her that I had once been a speechwriter for Ariel Sharon. And that's when, looking at her facial expression, I became concerned that her head might be about to blow up.

Among Palestinians, Sharon had probably been the most hated Israeli leader, and Samar probably hadn't expected one of his former underlings to show up in her office. I wanted to explain to her the random way that I had ended up in Israel in the first place, and that my own politics were far more dovish than the old general's had been. And that I wasn't even Israeli. But I wasn't sure if there was time for all that before I heard a popping sound and she was left headless. Her eyes were bugging out and her face looked pale. She backed up in her chair a little as she took in what I had just told her.

Just as I was about to try to assure her that I was not here to occupy her office, though, she began to calm down, apparently deciding that I was not necessarily her enemy. And we eased into a pleasant conversation, which began with me asking her about her job in the United States.

"It's always an uphill struggle," she said, "especially when trying to reach lawmakers and influential institutes. They're always flooded by the views of one side, and so our perspective is new to them, and scary."

Samar told me that several of the Palestine Center's board members advocated a single Palestinian state in all the land that currently comprised Israel and the Palestinian territories, but that her personal view was more moderate. She believed that the just solution entailed Israel withdrawing entirely behind the pre-1967 armistice lines—including from all of East Jerusalem and its holy sites—and that Palestinian refugees should be allowed to choose whether to return to their former homes in Israel.

"What do you think are the prospects for reaching those goals?" I asked.

"They're positive," she said, "because with the election of Netanyahu, the true face of Israel has been exposed. It shows the whole world what the Palestinians have been trying to say: We're the ones who don't have a partner for peace. At least now there's clarity.

"Israel doesn't have security because of its territorial appetite," she went on. "It's about territory, not terrorism."

For Samar, as for a lot of other Palestinians, Israel clearly used security concerns as a pretext to avoid having to give up territory. Even though growing settlements in the West Bank and an increasing Jewish presence in East Jerusalem stoked the rage that led to Palestinian terrorism, these forces showed no sign of abating.

I didn't agree with her that Israel's actions had nothing to do with the constant threats to its citizens' lives, but there was no denying that an influential segment of the Israeli population was mostly focused on holding on to territory. If Israel wanted to argue that its military actions and the restrictions it placed on the Palestinians didn't stem from at least some territorial appetite, the settlers were not helping its case.

"Do you think there are any signs of change in the U.S.?" I asked.

"It's still too early to tell with the new administration," she said, "but there is some change on the ground. The 'Israel can do no wrong, let's stand by her' mentality has changed. In the American Jewish community, it's now okay to criticize, and to say that criticism is in Israel's interests. That's also true on Capitol Hill, which will be helpful for the president when he has to take a tough position."

Presumably, what she meant by "a tough position" was needing to pressure Israel into making concessions that would supposedly help bring about a just resolution—the kind of thing prior administrations and congresses did not have the political cover to do.

I told Samar that I had been going through periods of doubt in my quest, and that the reason I had started it to begin with was fatigue with the Middle East situation. Did she ever feel the same sort of disheartening frustration? I asked.

"Yes," she said, without a moment's hesitation. "Especially when it's always the same people in control. On the Israeli side, the same faces come back again and again. On the Palestinian side, it's 'until death do us part' with our leaders."

When I asked her if she had any particular criticism for those on her side of the conflict, particularly of the extremists who used violence at every opportunity, she said that she most definitely did, but that it was Israeli aggressions and injustices that gave them their motivations and opportunities.

"What pushes you to keep going?" I asked.

She thought about it for a moment and then said, "It's not necessarily the positive things or the quiet times that remotivate me. Sometimes the things that disgust you also motivate you. For example, thinking about the lives of the children of Gaza."

I could tell that this was not merely rhetoric. She looked genuinely pained just thinking about their situations, and I didn't blame her: the children of Gaza truly had it rough. And in the end, any potential peacemaker had to be driven by coming to the aid of those—on both sides—who were suffering.

"The whole conflict is so male dominated," I said, thinking of Abby's success at PeaceMaker. "Do you think that if women had more of a role, the situation might be improved?"

Samar smiled and said, "I used to think that if women were in charge, things would be different, but then women like Thatcher come to mind. The only difference, I think, would be the style of negotiations. They would be less driven by ego than when men do it."

And speaking of ego, I had one last question for her.

"How can I personally solve the conflict?" I asked.

"Well, if you do," she began, "we won't be employed anymore."

I nodded. This would probably be a sad by-product of my success.

"I could say 'Get all sides to abide by UN resolutions,' but that sounds naïve," she went on. "And a lot of people like the idea of building trust and confidence incrementally, but that doesn't work. So just have Israel quit the territories, and then we'll work on understanding. It's the cold turkey approach."

When I got back from my meeting with Samar, I found a very odd email. It was from Brenda, the departmental assistant at the university where I taught classes. She said a middle-aged couple from Albany had shown up at the university, looking for me. There had to be some mistake, I thought. I didn't know anyone from Albany, and there was no reason a middle-aged couple from there should be trying to find me. I called Brenda to get some more information.

"They're very charming," she said to me, "that Rabbi Paskovitchi and his wife. And they want to have dinner with you and Abby tonight."

Brenda was young and from Kansas. They were a middle-aged Orthodox couple from New York State. The fact that she had clearly taken such an instant shine to the Paskovitchis was a little odd.

"Do it for me," she said. "They're very nice. At least call them."

I liked Brenda, and she seemed so intently interested in the Paskovitchis' happiness that I couldn't help agreeing to call them. But before I did, I checked something with Brenda.

"Yes," she said. "They want to take you *and* Abby to dinner."

They had clearly read my first book, in which I wrote about Abby. But I wasn't sure she would be so eager to get involved.

"Abby," I said after my call with Brenda, "do you have any interest in going to dinner with a middle-aged couple from Albany?"

"What?" she asked. "Who are they?"

"I don't really know," I said. "It's a rabbi and his wife. They must have read my book and they want to take us out for dinner."

I explained that I thought that there was always the possibility that the Paskovitchis might hold the key to Middle East peace. It would be irresponsible not to meet with them.

"But don't you think this is a little odd?" she asked.

"Of course I do, but Brenda thought we'd get along."

"With a middle-aged couple from Albany?"

"They're the Paskovitchis," I said. "They're not just any random middle-aged couple from Albany."

But Abby had a point. In fact, the more I thought about it, the weirder it seemed that the Paskovitchis—no matter how charming they were—would waltz in from out of town, show up at the university, and expect Abby and I to go to dinner with them that very night. Nevertheless, I decided to call them at the hotel they were staying at, unsure exactly what I was going to say.

"Hello," a male voice answered when I called the number Brenda had given me.

"Is this Rabbi Paskovitchi?"

"Gregory!" he boomed. "So good to hear from you!"

Do I know this guy? I wondered. I didn't remember him from anywhere, but he was acting like we were old friends.

"Thank you," I said. "Thank you for, um, coming to the university to find me."

"Of course," he answered. "We're in town from Albany and we thought we'd take the opportunity to finally meet you. We really enjoyed your book and we wanted to talk in person. In fact, I went ahead and made dinner reservations for the four of us for tonight. Abigail will be joining us, won't she?"

You already made dinner reservations? I thought. *We've never even met or communicated before today.*

"Well, she—"

"We want to talk to you about Israel," he said.

Of course you do, I thought.

159

I told him that dinner wasn't going to work—I legitimately did already have plans that night—but that I would be glad to meet him and his wife for coffee at their hotel the next day. Abby, however, wouldn't be able to make it.

When I met them at the hotel, they were exactly as Brenda had described them. Moshe, a middle-aged rabbi from Albany, and his wife Miriam.

And she had been right. They were extremely charming.

I liked the Paskovitchis immediately, and before I knew it, I had forgotten that this was an odd situation at all. Of course I was meeting with complete strangers who had just shown up at my office to discuss Israel. Why wouldn't I be?

They had been to Israel many times, they told me, and had even met some of the people I had written about in my first book.

"I wonder what his reaction was when he read that!" Miriam said, referring to one of the people whose charming eccentricities I had documented in my book. "He must have been proud. Or maybe embarrassed. It's hard to say, isn't it?"

I told her that I didn't know what anyone thought about anything. All I had tried to do in the book was to be as honest as possible about my own odd story.

"Let me ask you," the rabbi broke in, "did your experience in the Israeli government and at the UN make you more or less optimistic about the chances for peace?"

This was a question that I got a lot, and nobody was ever particularly happy with my answer.

"Less," I said.

There were a lot of reasons for this, of course, but I quickly went through some of them with the Paskovitchis: endless animosity, religious fundamentalism on both sides, Palestinian rejectionism, Israeli intransigence, and what often seemed like a total inability of everyone involved to do anything with any modicum of organization or planning.

What I didn't tell them was that on my return, I had had the idea that if the people back home in North America had been given the problem to solve they could have managed it—and that, for the most part, this hope had been squashed when I actually engaged with those people on the issues.

"What do you think?" I asked. "You seem to be pretty knowledgeable about the situation."

"I'm a religious person," he said, pointing at the skullcap on his head, "and I understand why Jews want to have control of Jerusalem and be able to live in parts of the West Bank that have biblical significance."

Oh, no, I thought. *This stuff.*

It seemed to me that whenever religion entered the conversation, there was almost no point in even continuing. When the two sides were talking about legal rights, political logistics, or even historical imperatives, it was possible to discuss substance and make some progress. But once it got into competing religious claims or contrary biblical narratives—about feeling a burning need to live in a specific geographic location because of, as he put it, its "biblical significance"—I never saw much hope of reconciliation.

But then Rabbi Paskovitchi surprised me.

"But when it comes to finally making peace," he continued, "I really don't think these things should play an important role."

I didn't hear this sort of thing often from religious people. I heard it from secular players in the debate, but when they said it, I didn't think it carried as much weight. When a religious person—a rabbi—said it, it was intriguing.

Maybe the Paskovitchis really were the key to making Middle East peace after all.

"But religious extremists are a big part of the problem," he said. "Extremists on both sides."

And Miriam nodded.

"It's just a shame," she added, "that they're always fighting about things in the sky, when there is so much on the ground that they could be working on together."

I nodded in full agreement. The Paskovitchis from Albany, I thought, were a breath of fresh air. They were not paranoid, not obsessive, not dogmatic, and not locked into any unbreakable ideology. Above all, they were pragmatic.

As our chat proceeded, I realized that they didn't have any particular questions they had been dying to ask, or a special agenda in meeting me. They didn't even have any forceful views that they wanted to tell me about, as so many did. They really did just want to hang out.

When our conversation was over, I thought that even if it had been somewhat strange, I was glad that I had met with them. And even if I still found it odd that they were so interested in talking about the Middle East that they had shown up at the university to see me, I thought that if there were more people like them involved in the debate—intelligent, broad-minded, light-hearted, and humane—there might be a little more hope. I had little doubt that if the Paskovitchis were given the reins of state-craft and peacemaking, they would make quick work of the situation in the Middle East.

Even so, when we walked together to the front doors of the hotel, the rabbi said something that took me aback a little.

"In the future," he said, "should we contact you on your cell?"

In the future? I thought. What was going to happen in the future? Did I have a *future* with the Paskovitchis?

I stared at them. They were smiling and jolly and sort of grandparently. And I couldn't help but picture our future together. Then Miriam told me something that only extended this bizarre line of thinking further.

"Remember," she said, "you'll always have a second home in Albany."

"You should totally take advantage of that," Luke said, when I told him what had happened. "A second home in Albany is not something to turn your back on."

I rolled my eyes. Sometimes I got the feeling that our entire friendship was based on Luke mocking me.

"You should just show up there at the beginning of the sum-mer," he said, "and tell them that from now on you'll be 'sum-mering in Albany.' Then stay for two months. Maybe the road to peace goes through Albany."

I shook my head. I had passed through Albany a couple of times, and I didn't find this likely.

"Maybe they showed up because they're obsessed with the Middle East," Luke said, "or maybe they're just people with nothing better to do—like you."

And as entertaining as Luke seemed to find making light of my project, I still thought that there was something encouraging about the Paskovitchis. It wasn't just that I agreed with them on many issues—hopefully it wasn't, anyway. It was also that they were able to listen to and understand arguments from many directions and, even more important, they were able to avoid dehumanizing and degrading those who they did not agree with. It was a shame there were not more Paskovitchis among the stakeholders in the debate.

"It sounds like you're sort of obsessed with these people," Luke said.

"They're very charming," I told him.

Luke didn't realize, I thought, what a contrast the Paskovitchis were to some of the other people I regularly came into contact with. The professionals were generally fine, with a few exceptions, but the run of the mill hobbyist pundits who constantly emailed me and showed up at my book events, all of whom seemed to think that they could solve the conflict in six months or less without even leaving their apartments, all of whom had nothing better to do—they were mostly unbearable.

The Lion Claws. The Harold C Funks. And the Ted Collinses.

And then something unsettling occurred to me. I didn't know

why it had never crossed my mind before, and I felt stupid because it hadn't, but Luke's last name was Collins.

Could Luke and Ted Collins be related?

"Wait," I said. "You're not related to *Ted* Collins, are you?"

Luke paused and smiled.

"Uh, he's my father."

I was startled, and unsure what to say. Ted Collins was one of the most active Middle East internet warriors I had encountered. He ran a popular right-wing blog that pushed extreme positions pretty similar to Lion Claw's, but he was far more influential. He had an extensive mailing list, numbering, I'd heard, in the tens of thousands, and a well trafficked website that occasionally even got noticed by the media. Recently, for example, I'd read an article in a major magazine tearing into Collins for his important role in the campaign of personal attacks targeting Obama.

Collins was one of the most active purveyors of the anti-Obama vitriol. Several times a week he would write articles of his own—or post articles of other right-wing hobbyist pundits—and send them out to his list. Generally, they alleged that Obama had anti-Semitic intentions, or that he was going to bring about Israel's ruin. He also went beyond this to some of the other attacks being floated. Obama was secretly Muslim, for example, or he was not eligible to be president because he had been born abroad and his birth certificate had been forged.

This was Luke's father? How did I not know this? Why had he never told me, as I moved forward in my current project—or before, when I'd been working in the Israeli government?

Then it occurred to me: Maybe the reason Luke had been so mocking of me trying to make peace, I thought, was because he had long had to deal with his father's own attempts at dealing with the Middle East—as out there as they were. In fact, as I sat there in front of Luke, flabbergasted, it occurred to me that in all the years I had known Luke, I could only remember him mentioning his father once. We had been talking about books and literature, and Luke had mentioned that when he had been a little boy his father had often read Shakespeare to him before bed, working their way through most of his plays. That was it. I didn't think that Luke had mentioned him even one other time. Why had he been so tight-lipped about his dad? And the idea that the same man who used to read his son Shakespeare—an image that to me bespoke liberalism and broad-mindedness—sent out emails so offensive as to be almost libelous was astounding.

"Really?" I asked Luke. "Ted Collins is your father? Ted Collins, the—"

And suddenly I was unsure what I should say. Luke seldom spoke about the Middle East, and I wasn't sure what he thought of his father or his father's politics. I didn't want to insult him, but this was now murky terrain.

"The, uh—" I said.

"Yeah?"

"Well, I wouldn't say 'psycho,' exactly, but he's a little . . . out there."

"How do you know him?"

"I don't," I told him, "I mean, not personally, but I come across his . . . work . . . now and then. And I get his emails."

Luke started laughing.

"Oh, no," he said, actually slapping the table. "You get those emails?"

I nodded, and he laughed more.

"How did you get on his list?"

"I'm not sure."

"Well," he said. "Once you're on, you can never get off."

"I've noticed."

"No," Luke told me, suddenly seeming a bit less amused. "I'm serious. I've tried to get off that list many times. It's impossible. Once you're on, you're stuck."

"Well, what do you think of his activities?" I asked.

"I don't know," he said. "I mean, I personally think that he may have a real psychological problem when it comes to the Middle East. I think he's obsessive about it. You know, before this he was really, really into researching the real history of Jesus, and now he's really, really into the Middle East. I think it could be sort of compulsive or escapist."

He went on in this vein for a while, getting at something a bit sad—that his father might use the Middle East as a sort of crutch to help him cope with some emptiness or frustration in his own life.

"First it was the historical Jesus," he said again. "Now this."

This idea was interesting, I thought, and a possibility. In fact, I wondered if maybe this same analysis could be applied to some of the other obsessive voices always chiming in when it came to the situation in the Middle East. Obviously not the professionals—although maybe it was possible that the same

could be said for some of them—but perhaps for all the scream-
ing voices on the left and the right, the Ted Collinses and the
Harold C Funks, there were psychological needs that drove their
focus on a place that was so far away and so far removed from
their daily lives.

"Do you think your dad would be willing to meet with me?"
I asked.

"Probably, but I'm not sure I'd recommend it."

"But I could email him and—"

"If you start emailing him," Luke said, "I recommend getting
a dedicated email address for it—otherwise he'll overwhelm you
completely."

Then Luke half-smiled, and I wasn't sure if I was imagining
it or not, but it seemed to me like maybe I had touched a patch
of hidden sadness in my old friend—if maybe Luke was thinking
about how those days of his father reading him Shakespeare had
faded away completely.

A little nervous about what his reaction might be, I emailed Ted
Collins and introduced myself. Now that I knew he was Luke's
father, this felt especially odd.

"I hold regular gatherings at my house for a small group of
zealots," he wrote back immediately. "Maybe you could join us
for one of them."

A small group of zealots? I thought.

I really wasn't sure I wanted to attend one of these "gatherings," but was definitely curious about what went on at them.

"Oh, those things," Luke said, when I told him about it later. "Yeah, I heard about them. I'd stay away if I were you."

I decided that it might be more productive to meet with Ted one-on-one than in the company of his "small group of zealots," and I emailed him to see if he would be interested in meeting for coffee. I didn't mention his "small group of zealots," but sort of hoped that he wouldn't bring them along.

While I waited for him to respond, I pictured the scene if he did bring them with him to the Starbucks where we might meet.

Ted, his zealots, and I would stand in line at the counter.

"What can I get for you?" the barista would ask us.

"I'll have a coffee," I'd say.

"We'll have a united Jerusalem as the eternal capital of the Jewish people forever!" the zealots would shout in unison.

When Ted Collins responded to me, though, he gave no indication that he planned to bring his band of zealots with him. I was pretty relieved, and we set a time to meet. Luke, meanwhile, was amused by this turn of events, but was not without some words of warning.

"Talking politics with my father in a public place," he said, "can be an . . . interesting . . . experience. Be careful."

I wasn't eager to be involved in any kind of public scene, where racist or violent statements were being thrown around—which seemed possible, given some of the positions taken in Ted Collins's internet writing—and as the date of our meeting approached, Luke's warning echoed in my mind.

When he arrived at the coffee shop, he didn't have a retinue of zealots with him, which I thought was a good start to a productive conversation. As we shook hands, I tried to decide if he looked like Luke.

"I'm trying to make peace in the Middle East," I told him when he sat down, "and so I'm speaking to people from all along the political spectrum. Which is why I wanted to speak to you."

At this, Ted laughed a little. It was apparent that he knew just where he fit on the spectrum. And as we began to get into substance, it was clear he was perfectly comfortable there. He was disarmingly soft-spoken and genteel, but his opinions were razor-edged.

Now that Obama was president, I asked him, did he have any second thoughts about all the negative allegations he had made about him during the campaign?

"Every single thing I said about Obama was true," he said, "and I still believe everything. Obama is a Muslim and since he is not a natural born citizen, he is not eligible to be president."

"What do you make of it when people say that sort of talk is racist?" I asked.

He waved that off.

"Leftists," he said, "trot out racism to shut you up."

I didn't have much interest in getting into an extended discussion with him about the politics around the president, so I switched directions and asked him what he thought of the latest Middle East trends.

"They're moving to the point where it's possible to strong-

arm Israel," he said. "And all this is planned. Someone is machinating, and they're building up a lot of steam."

Anytime someone starts talking about mysterious forces
"machinating," I start to get uncomfortable with the conversation. But I pressed on a bit, asking who "they" were. He was
happy to expand on it. The *New York Times,* the State Department, the United Nations, Barack Obama, and a good portion of
the Democratic Party.

"What do you think of J-Street?" I asked.

"I hate them," he said.

I stared at him, expecting him to continue or explain his
hatred. But he just stared back at me. He hated them, and that's
all there was to it.

"Okay," I said, looking over at the people next to us to see if
they were listening. "So on the Middle East, what do you think
the solution to it all is?"

"Well, first of all," he said, "there is no political solution.
If there is a solution, there's only a military solution. But there
probably is no solution. We just have to manage the situation.
Why do we need a solution?"

I had heard this sort of argument before, and as far as I understood it, it meant solidifying the status quo in the most tenable fashion possible. At best, I thought, this was a pessimistic
approach that was doomed to fail in the long run—the status quo
simply was not sustainable. At worst, it seemed like a sinister
move by the more powerful side to maintain its position at the
expense of the other side.

"Well, surely," I said, "you must agree that the situation is not good. That there are injustices on both sides."

"When people go on about the injustices done to the Palestinians, it drives me up the wall," he said. "The Palestinians would rather remain stateless. It gives them good income, with no responsibilities."

I tried to take this in, thinking about all the Palestinian children I knew were suffering at this moment—about the children of Gaza that Samar Assad had mentioned. If Ted knew that I was thinking this, I thought, he would immediately consider me weak, naïve, or misled.

"So what do you want?" I asked. "Or rather, what do you think should happen?"

"The whole narrative has to be changed," he said. "Israel has legitimate rights, and too many people forget that. We need to start talking about rights, and stop talking about security."

Presumably, what he meant by this was the whole debate should not turn on protecting Israeli and Palestinian lives, as much as it should on an abstract, almost academic sense of who was entitled to what. For Ted, Israel had historical and legal rights to all the land it held, and continuing to make use of those rights was an imperative that went beyond any pragmatic concerns.

Wow, I thought. *I wouldn't rush to tell the people actually living in the Middle East that they should forget about their security.*

"So how should I make peace?" I asked.

"The Palestinians won't compromise at all, and we shouldn't compromise," he said, "so you might as well try to grow a third leg. It's not happening."

*   *   *

As I walked away after our conversation, I found myself think-ing that he was different from the persona that came across in his online output. The same extremist ideas were there, but the way he voiced them in person was starkly different. He was articulate and laid-back and I could even sense a wry sense of humor—and in these things I could see his son Luke. I wondered what Ted had thought of our conversation.

A few days later, I was sitting with Luke at a pub, and he was able to tell me.

"He thinks he convinced you," Luke said. "On everything."

I smiled and sipped from my beer. This was not the case, but it was intriguing to hear that this was the impression Ted Collins had gotten from our conversation. I wondered aloud how many others of the people I had come in contact with felt the same thing. Samar Assad? Stephen Walt? Abe Foxman? Lion Claw? Harold C Funk?

"I guess everyone thinks their own views are totally reason-able," I said, "and that they're impossible to argue against effec-tively. Nobody thinks they're crazy."

Luke nodded.

"No," he said. "Not even you."

CHAPTER TEN

Nice Jewish Boys with Guns

I had met up with my Israeli friend Amir, updating him on my latest activities, and he had given me some bad news: the Dutch anti-Israel activist refused to meet with me.

"It's weird," he said. "She won't shut up about Israel most of the time, but she doesn't want to speak to you."

This was disappointing. It was one thing to have power players like former presidents brushing me off . . . but usually it was just this sort of random fringe persons who bombarded me with their opinions. I wasn't sure what to make of this.

And the fact was that, from what Amir had told me, I thought she represented a voice in the debate that I hadn't really tapped into yet. The extreme semiorganized Left. So I decided that if for whatever reason she wasn't going to speak to me, I needed to contact her compatriots.

One of the most active and controversial groups on that side of the spectrum was called the International Solidarity Movement, which brought volunteers together to protest the Israeli occupation and try to obstruct the Israeli military's actions against the Palestinians, and used all their energy and resources to promote the Palestinian case around the world. I thought it wouldn't hurt to give them a call to say hello.

The ISM had branches all over the United States and in Europe, where it had especially strong support. In fact, although its main activities were focused in the Middle East itself, a good deal of the ISM's resources and visibility came from its links to supporters from abroad—and several of its most visible activists and leaders were American.

One of the incidents that had brought the ISM into the spotlight, in fact, involved a twenty-three-year-old American girl from Washington State named Rachel Corrie. Corrie had come to the Middle East to volunteer for the ISM, undergone their training, and then participated in their resistance efforts against the Israeli Army. Acting as a human shield, she had stood between an Israeli bulldozer and a Palestinian home the Israelis were about to demolish—as part of their policy of demolishing Palestinian property they believe is being used to aid terrorism.

Israel said that what happened next was an accident, that the bulldozer driver hadn't seen Corrie blocking his way. The ISM said that it was intentional, and proceeded to use Corrie's fate as a PR tool. Regardless of who was right, Rachel Corrie had been run over and killed.

When I called and emailed the ISM offices in Massachusetts, Florida, and Northern California, I got no response from anyone, so I decided to contact the UK offices. Apparently, though, they were busy operating a training course for volunteers heading off for Palestine. So that's why I started trying to reach the ISM's people in Ramallah.

Between wrong numbers and outdated numbers, it took me a long while to track down the ISM, and in the meantime it seemed like I was talking to half the population of Ramallah. I felt like a telemarketer with absolutely no grasp of the local language.

"Is this the International Solidarity Movement?" I asked one person who answered her phone.

"English no!" she said, and then added a long string of words in Arabic, none of which I understood.

Not sure how to respond, I resorted to the only sentence I knew in Arabic.

"I am studying Arabic at New York University," I said in Arabic, trying to be careful to get the intonation right on each word.

When I was done, there was silence at the other end of the line. The woman who had had the unfortunate luck to answer my call didn't know how to deal with a stranger with an odd accent who had apparently called to announce what classes he was taking in school.

I suddenly remembered how to say "thank you" in Arabic.

"Shukran," I said.

"Afwan," she responded politely, and I smiled. Me and this stranger in Ramallah had had a moment.

After a lot of calls sort of like that, I finally got through by email to the ISM's media coordinator in the West Bank, and explained what I was up to. She said that she'd be happy to talk, but that it might be better if I spoke to Neta Golan, one of the cofounders of the ISM, who lived in Ramallah. Then she signed off her email, "In solidarity, Sasha."

I thanked her by email, and signed off "In solidarity indeed, Gregory."

Then I called Neta Golan, a renegade Israeli who, along with her Palestinian comrades, ran the ISM.

Now here's the thing: I came to the subject of the ISM with some undeniable prejudice against the organization, since I had heard so many horrible things about them—not just from my time working with the Israelis, but also in the media since then. Despite that, I really wanted to give them a chance to share their side of the story, and was determined to stay as open-minded and neutral as possible as I heard them out. I would hear about their activities and philosophy from their own mouths, and make up my own mind about them.

The only problem was that when I got through to Neta Golan in Ramallah, she wasn't particularly eager to open up to me.

"Well, what's your background?" she asked, when I tried to jump into a conversation about her and her organization. "Tell me about yourself first."

All I could think about at this moment was the face of Samar Assad (of the Palestine Center) when I had told her that I had worked for Ariel Sharon. Neta Golan was actually Israeli, but she was probably even more firmly enmeshed in the ground game of Palestinian nationalism than Samar and her colleagues. What would Neta think when I told her about my past? Would she want to share anything at all? Would her head explode, as I had been worried that Samar's might?

But I figured that hiding things from her wouldn't work, and so I just decided to tell her everything. I told her about how I had stumbled into the Israeli government, and about some of my experiences in it. I told her about how I had started doing some Middle East journalism after that, and about all the cranks that this had brought out of the woodwork and in my direction. I told her about my first book, and about how rather than it being my exit from the Middle East, it had only made me the target of new loudmouths of all stripes. And I told her about my current quest to personally put the whole conflict behind us, and about the people I had been speaking to and the things I had been doing.

Eventually, I found myself pouring out a little more information than was probably necessary. I started telling her that I had sporadic doubts that I was progressing much, but that occasional moments—like when Yossi Beilin had seemed to take me seriously, and when I had met with the exceedingly charming Paskovitchis from Albany—gave me hope for the future. It was when I started to mention the Paskovitchis that I decided maybe I should stop rambling on.

But although I had opened up to Golan, she wasn't ready to do the same.

"I'm going to have to google you," she said, "to check up on you before we talk."

Google me? I thought. *But I just told you everything there is to know.* There really wasn't a whole lot more that she would be able to find online. She would come across people from both the Right and the Left criticizing me, but I wasn't particularly worried about her uncovering anything else.

So when a couple of days passed and I hadn't heard from her, it began to disturb me. I had told her everything. What had she found that so offended her that she didn't want to talk to me?

I contacted Sasha, the ISM's media coordinator, and asked her what was going on. Would she talk to me like she had offered?

No, she'd now have to consult with Neta, she said, before she could talk to me.

And when a couple more days passed and I hadn't heard back from either of them, I thought the message was clear. The ISM was not interested in talking to me. This just left me with a continuing negative sense of the organization, based on all the secondhand reports I'd heard—many of which suggested that even if it was not directly in league with them, the ISM indirectly aided the activities of violent Palestinian extremists. I just wished they had agreed to give me their side of the story.

When the phone call from the White House finally came, I managed to miss it. And not for any important reason either. I wasn't talking with the premier of Russia or negotiating a deal with a Saudi envoy. No, when the phone call from the White House finally came, I was out back, showing some friends a birdhouse Abby and I had recently received as a gift.

I was delighted that Kevin had actually called me—I was really rolling now—but the message he left for me said that he was at the airport on his way "overseas," so I should try to reach him in the next few minutes. When I called him back, of course, I only got his voice mail.

Overseas?

He was probably jetting off for some secret meeting in Syria, or to lay the groundwork for covert negotiations with Hamas. And here I was showing off my new birdhouse.

Anxious to see if Kevin had perhaps also emailed me, I rushed to my computer, but found only a couple of new emails from Lion Claw and one from Jacob, my friend in Israel. Jacob was going to be coming home to visit soon, and he wanted Abby and I to go with him to some kind of "flower-themed party." That sounded terrible, and after what had just happened with the missed call, I wasn't really in the mood to read the whole email, so I just scanned it briefly and put it aside for the moment.

If the International Solidarity Movement was made up of what might be considered left-wing extremists, the Jewish Defense League was made up of their opposite numbers on the Right. But while the ISM had given me the brush-off, the JDL readily agreed to meet with me, and soon after the birdhouse incident I was on my way to one of their offices.

The office was in a building in a suburban neighborhood that housed a variety of Jewish organizations. There were offices for Jewish camps, Jewish charities, and Jewish women's groups—and, sticking out a bit from these down-to-earth outfits—there was the Jewish Defense League.

Founded in 1968 by Meir Kahane, a young New York rabbi, the JDL had amassed thousands of members within a few years and was immediately a controversial organization because of its violent, uncompromising bent. In its heyday, it concentrated on confronting anti-Semitism—through actual physical violence, at times—and in combating the Soviet Union's refusal to allow its Jews to emigrate. To further the latter goal, it had gone as far as bombing Soviet property in the United States. And when tensions between New York's black and Jewish populations had been at a boiling point, it had even physically tangled with the Black Panthers.

When Kahane moved to Israel, where he founded a movement that was outlawed by the Israeli government and was barred from running for the Israeli parliament, the JDL began to lose energy and momentum—even as its ideological offspring among the Israeli settlers in the West Bank continued to flourish and grow powerful. And after Kahane was assassinated in 1990 by a Muslim extremist allegedly connected to al-Qaeda, the JDL's American presence steadily dropped off the map in terms of relevance.

But immediately after September 11, and in the years since, it seemed to have had something of a resurgence, not just of the main group, but also of various splinter and copycat groups. Right after the terrorist attacks in 2001, in fact, a guy I'd met at NYU had approached me at school and asked me if I wanted to join an impromptu vigilante organization. It had been set up because there were fears—and concrete threats—that Jewish neighborhoods in Brooklyn were going to be targeted by Arab terrorists upset about events in the Middle East and energized by the recent disaster in downtown Manhattan.

The vigilante organization wanted to protect the Jews of Brooklyn, apparently not trusting the NYPD or the federal government to do it.

"All these guys are doing," the NYU kid told me, "is patrolling the neighborhoods, with one arm inside a gym bag holding a rifle, in case there are any incidents."

I politely declined.

But now I was going to be meeting with another man named Meir, a senior member of the JDL who had been close to Meir Kahane himself.

I waited in the lobby of the building, as we had arranged, and I watched a few older Jewish women come into the building and go up on the elevator.

When Meir walked in, he was unmistakable. In contrast to the others, he looked less like the kind of person who enjoyed watching daytime TV and more like the kind of person who enjoyed smashing TVs with his head "just to test" if he still had it.

He was into his fifties, but gave off the impression that he spent enough time in the gym—or just smashing things with his head—to ensure that he stayed in good physical shape.

"Gregory?" he asked, and put out a big hand for me to shake. I might have been imagining it, but the look in his eyes seemed to say, "If you are an anti-Semite, my plan is to eat your heart."

I shook his hand and tried to give off a wholly Semitic vibe.

He led me into the elevator and then down a long hallway to a one-room office beside the offices for a Jewish summer camp. There were some picket signs against one wall and files, boxes, and assorted other clutter scattered around the room.

The JDL was planning a protest against the Obama administration's Middle East policies the next day, and Meir told me that he thought it would go smoothly. He said that at a recent event, though, things had gone badly.

"I brought specific people," he said. "Big guys. And when we took a photograph of the opposing protestors, one of them pushed me. So we crushed his glasses and started mangling his head."

Mangling his head?

"How are the JDL's operations seen by the police?" I asked.

"There are all kinds of lies and deceptions from the cops," he said. "But in the end, the only language the enemies of the Jews understand is the JDL. And we advocate not one inch of retreat."

It was not exactly clear to me what he meant by "the only language the enemies of the Jews understand is the JDL," but it sure sounded ominous.

As our conversation progressed, Meir told me that in the old days, some of his time had been spent hunting Nazi war criminals.

"Did you ever catch any?" I asked.

He smiled and said, "We took care of some of them."

"Today, though," I said, "what percentage of your activity is Israel related?"

"Everything," he said. "Anti-Zionism is the new anti-Judaism."

The JDL was currently involved in a number of endeavors: holding protests against what it felt were unfair policies of the Obama administration, going to anti-Israel protests and getting into actual physical fights with the protestors, threatening those it perceived as enemies of the Jewish state, and sending its foot soldiers as unsolicited "security" to Jewish and Israel-related events.

I brought up the fact that some Israelis I had spoken to in the past, including in the Israeli government, didn't appreciate the JDL's activities or find them helpful. He brushed this off.

"I don't know if they're behind us or not behind us," he said, "but I don't know why they would not be behind us. What we're doing is wonderful."

"How should I make peace?" I asked.

"There will no be peace," he answered. "We do not have a peace plan. Anyone who presents a plan is a demagogue. Israel should get it through its head that we're in this for the long haul."

On that bright note, I decided to wrap this up. But just then, Meir's phone rang and he answered it.

"Yes," he said to whoever was on the phone, "but you need to be in very good shape."

Then he paused, listening.

"Well," he continued. "Because what we do is very difficult."

When he hung up the phone, I pressed him on what that call had been about. Apparently, the JDL was patrolling Jewish neighborhoods to protect against terrorism aimed at Jews here in North America, and to make sure that their people on patrol were able to handle the combat they seemed to imagine could break out at any moment, they were training them in martial arts.

"Can I come to a training class?" I asked, expecting him to demur.

"Sure," he said, nodding and smiling. "And would you like one of our T-shirts?"

As I took a T-shirt from him, I wondered if I was going to end up on some kind of cockamamie patrol through a suburban neighborhood. I was prepared for anything, though, and that's how, a few days later, I found myself doing combat training with the Jewish Defense League.

It had been a long time since I'd done much physical activity, and I had no idea how I'd be able to handle this training—or what I was in store for. But, wearing gym clothes, I showed up at the training center, where I found an odd assortment of characters waiting for me.

There was a very old man with a long white beard and some weird pouches hanging on strings around his neck, a kid who looked no older than seventeen, a large man wearing an army hat, an old woman who seemed to be talking to a wall, and a young African-American woman.

Was I in the wrong place? *This* was the Jewish Defense League?

At first I thought this motley crew was engaged in a lively conversation, but after standing there for a few seconds, I was able to parse out what was actually happening:

1. The old woman really was talking to the wall, or to the air, or to herself. I couldn't make out anything she was actually saying, but the rest of them were ignoring her.
2. The big guy wearing the army hat and the old man were staying silent, staring at the floor.
3. The African-American woman and the kid were involved in an animated conversation about how the kid's sister had recently called off her engagement to her fiancé.

I tried to picture this group doing any kind of paramilitary patrol, and came up short. Meanwhile, I noticed, all of them had begun looking at me strangely, as if I were wearing a sombrero and a ballroom dress.

What? I thought. *I'm the weird one?*

I smiled uncomfortably but didn't say anything. And for the next five minutes or so, I just stood there while the two conversations continued—the old woman talking to the wall, and the two younger people speaking about the broken engagement.

And, arguably, the weirdest part about the whole thing was the manner in which the African-American woman spoke. Needless to say, she didn't strike me as the quintessential Jew, and so I found it odd that she was at the Jewish Defense League, but when she spoke, she peppered her speech with Yiddish words and extremely clichéd Jewishisms that made her sound like she might have been someone who played bridge with my grandparents.

"She schlepped all the way there!" she exclaimed. "At least he could have been a mensch about the whole thing. Oy! What chutzpah!"

I couldn't quite believe this was coming from a young person, let alone an African-American young person who didn't look Jewish at all. She sounded like she was auditioning for a part in an all-black version of *Fiddler on the Roof.*

Finally, after I thought I really might be in the wrong place—though I couldn't imagine what purpose might have reasonably brought this group together in any circumstances—Meir walked in, followed by about a dozen big guys who looked like they might have just come from a violent protest and be on their way to another one, with just this class as a break between the two.

I guess those of us waiting here are the B-listers, I thought.

In fact, as we walked into the training room, the class instructor, who had come in with Meir, picked up on the fact that there was something amiss with the old woman and that perhaps she was not suited for advanced combat classes—and he suggested to her that she just watch the class instead of participating in it.

As we waited for the class to begin, a few more people filtered in, and I overheard a couple of them nearby me get into a conversation. One of them was a very muscular guy in a tank top. The other was a girl in her early twenties wearing a JDL T-shirt like the one Meir had given me. They apparently knew each other.

"Yeah, that guy was a total idiot," the man said. "I tried to explain to him that it's pretty obvious that Barack Obama is anti-Israel and just wants to crush it, and he just couldn't get it."

The girl nodded with a knowing smile.

"Just another self-hating Jew," she said.

Before we started, Meir went up to the front of the class, stood beside the instructor, and gave a short speech about what we were learning and why. It was a bit confusing but involved that particular week's reading from the Bible, an anecdote about a time when he had confronted a gun-wielding neo-Nazi, the Iranian nuclear program, and the martial arts exercises we were about to partake in. It was an unlikely cocktail, and I had some trouble following the logic, but there was apparently some connection between our martial arts practice and obstructing the Iranians' weaponization of their civilian nuclear program.

The class itself was less intense than I had imagined. It didn't compare at all to the security courses I had done in Israel, where among many other unpleasant experiences, I had been made to box the jujitsu champion of Israel while I had a loaded handgun lodged in my pocket.

Even so, it was still clear that they took what they were doing seriously. It wasn't sport martial arts or exercise. It was designed purely for combat purposes, and that was the sole reason the people of the JDL were engaged in it. We punched, kicked, and clawed, and imagined scenarios where we would use these skills.

And afterward I went back to my apartment ready for battle, or at least for a nap.

Later, I did a little more online research on the JDL, which had received a lot of negative attention over the years. According to some reports, they were considered a terrorist organization by the FBI. In 2001, its leaders Irv Ruben and Earl Krugel were allegedly caught planning bombings of a California mosque and of the office of an Arab-American congressman. And Baruch Goldstein, the American-born Israeli who had killed 29 Muslims and wounded 150 more in a shooting spree in Hebron in 1994, had been a member of the JDL before he had immigrated to Israel.

The JDL had also spawned a number of spinoff groups, including one that ran a serious paramilitary training camp in rural New York, teaching recruits classes in martial arts, firearms, and explosives, as well as politics and religion. It wasn't directly connected to the JDL, but there was also an extremist organization that maintained a public list of alleged enemies of Israel. It even listed locations and photographs of some of them, making the implicit suggestion that people take action against the people on the list—perhaps even violent action.

The list was extensive. It included actual extremists on the other side of the spectrum, but it also included Israeli academics, journalists, and rabbis. All of them, apparently, were enemies of the Jewish state. Somewhat inexplicably, it even had several Israeli leaders, including Ariel Sharon, because of his decision to withdraw from Palestinian land.

Yes, they were attacking Ariel Sharon from the *right*.

As I read through the list, I even discovered one of my own old law school professors was on it, along with Woody Allen, Richard Dreyfuss, and Thomas Friedman. There were also countless private citizens who had apparently crossed the line in some unidentified way.

I stared at the list for a while, having trouble believing it. Were they just talk, or were they really capable of harming those on the list?

I didn't know, but a few days later I had a meeting with a man who had encountered the same sort of people who were behind the list—and had come away with death threats. His name was Jeffrey Dvorkin, and he had a long and distinguished career in journalism, in both the theoretical and practical sides of the field. In 2000, he was asked to be National Public Radio's first ombudsman. They needed one, he told me, mostly because of the Middle East.

"Then nine-eleven happened and everything changed," he

said. "Along with the Second Intifada breaking out, it was a one-two punch to American journalism, and it allowed extreme voices on the pro-Israel side to come out."

He paused, then added, "It was like someone opened up an Uzi on me."

Dvorkin told me that whenever NPR would run a story on the Middle East situation—and in those difficult days, that was almost daily—they would be bombarded by emails and phone calls accusing its reporters and producers of anti-Semitic bias against Israel. Dvorkin himself, he said, would be the target of a great deal of it.

"They saved my job on a number of occasions," he said, "by calling for my resignation."

He smiled as he told me this, but I could tell that he was not amused by the memories. That the scars from it all had not yet healed.

"At one point," he went on, "they launched a 'Write Dvorkin' campaign."

The goal of the campaign had been to voice anger and disappointment with NPR's supposedly anti-Israel bias, and to make Dvorkin its prime target.

"They put a full-page ad in the *New York Times*, and I was the only one named in it," he said, pausing for a second and then adding, "I have it framed."

Then Dvorkin started telling me about something that sounded strangely familiar. A doctor, he said, had started sending him "insane emails."

"They were vituperative, angry, and threatening," he said.

A doctor? I thought. *Was he from New York? Was he a psychiatrist? Was his name Lion Claw?*

But no. He was from Pittsburgh, and he was a pediatric oncologist. Evidently, there were a number of these highly politicized doctors.

"Once," Dvorkin said, "I was doing a town hall–type discussion at a synagogue in Potomac, Maryland, and the doctor showed up and he just took over the whole meeting. The rabbi who had been onstage with me ran away, and for three and a half straight hours people were just pouring out invective at me."

Dvorkin told me that because of all the anger being directed at NPR, he was tasked with doing town halls in other cities too, to try to placate the people unhappy with NPR's coverage. The worst such event, he said, was in Boston, where the local NPR affiliate had lost a million dollars in funding because of all the anger about reporting that they believed slanted unfairly against Israel. Some even referred to NPR as "National Palestinian Radio." A thousand people came to the meeting, he said, to see him and a colleague answer questions about NPR's coverage of the Middle East.

"In addition to state troopers, I was protected by stocky, bulgy guys with short haircuts and overcoats," he said—and I smiled, because I had encountered my share of guys like that. "And during the talk, one person rushed the stage to attack my colleague."

But that wasn't as heated as things got. Dvorkin told me the culmination of his entanglement with the Middle East conflict was when the death threats started coming in.

"The phone calls would come in every Sunday night at one in the morning," he said, "and the voice on the other end would say things like 'We know where you live,' and 'You won't be able to do this much longer.'"

Eventually the FBI had to be called in, and after they had tracked the calls to a phone booth on the side of the I-95, they'd positioned a local cop car next to it each Sunday night, and the calls stopped.

But the experience didn't seem to have left Dvorkin.

"This was not about me or about NPR," he said. "It was about something much deeper."

This was a man who had felt the dangers of going up against some of the groups I'd been encountering. It was distressing, I thought, that these dangers weren't only to people taking part in the Middle East debate. Even the people reporting about it were vulnerable.

Anonymous death threats from the side of the highway? The FBI? And I thought the array of odd messages *I* got were disturbing. Compared to Dvorkin's story, they were nothing.

But when I got a new email the next morning, I was a bit more unsettled by it than I normally would be. The sender, whose name was Marcel, had read my first book, and he apparently hadn't cared for it much. The email said:

> I read your book and you can feel fine. You are not Jewish and
> not any of your ancestors. No Jew would write or think what you

wrote on page 24 on media, Holocaust, and Jews (not even as humor). You are a 100% Goy. By the way, the rest of the book is quite OK.

Obviously, this was absolutely trivial compared to what Dvorkin had experienced, but in light of my conversation with him, I now felt particularly sensitive to this sort of thing and didn't appreciate the way the letter was aimed not only at me, but also at my family.

In any case, I had to assume that in his second sentence, when Marcel seemed to be assuring me that I was not any of my *own* ancestors, he had worded something incorrectly. Being one or more of my own ancestors would have made for some very confusing family reunions, and probably been illegal in some states.

So Marcel was just assuring me that, because of a joke I'd made in my first book—of the kind, by the way, that can be seen on Israeli television essentially every night: I'd joked about "Jews controlling the media" and about Holocaust revisionism—neither I nor any of my family could possibly be Jewish. ("Goy" is a word for Gentile widely considered derogatory.) This would have no doubt come as quite a shocker to my fairly religious grandparents, my uncle who had voiced his own problems with my writing, or my grandfather's entire family—who lay in mass graves in Lithuania after having been murdered in the Holocaust. What a surprise it would have been to those murdered relatives that they were apparently there just because of a misunderstanding.

I was glad, though, that Marcel thought the rest of the book was "quite OK." He seemed like the kind of guy who was probably a top-notch literary critic. And maybe he would read my next one after all.

In a way, though, Marcel's email revitalized my thinking on my quest. We had all heard enough and had enough not only of the endless conflict, but also of all the extremist loudmouths and instigators on this side of the ocean who used it as a vehicle for channeling their own aggression, hatred, and racism.

So much time and energy was spent on infighting, finger-pointing, and personal point-scoring, when the truth was that everyone's energy would be better spent talking rationally about the actual issues. In doing so, everyone would hopefully begin to acknowledge that buried in all the rancor and violence, there had to be some sliver of shared humanity to be found. If peace was ever going to come to that cursed scrap of Middle Eastern earth, all parties were going to have acknowledge their own responsibilities and each other's rights. And to accept that not everyone had to agree with you.

My time had almost run out on this project, but I was not quite done yet. I had to make my final attempt at actually doing something constructive. I had spoken—or tried to speak—to a lot of different people who were in some way involved with the Middle East debate, and now it was time to try to put it all into practice. To decide what had to be done, and to try to convince the parties involved to implement it.

I had to make one last trip to Washington DC. I made dozens of emails and phone calls to people in DC as I prepared to go—diplomats, academics, journalists, and officials in the U.S. government, as well as at the Israeli Embassy and the Palestinian Mission. I was coming there to finally make peace, I told them all.

And I started to pack my bag. Clothes, some books, and the notes I had taken in the months that I had been peacemaking. And lying on top of all that, I put one item to bring me luck.

My PeaceMaker boxer shorts.

CHAPTER ELEVEN

With All Due Respect, You Must Be on Crack

I received the following email from a former Mossad officer whom I had arranged to meet in a hotel lobby:

> I'll be naked and carrying a TIME magazine—I repeat—I'll be carrying a TIME magazine.

I reread that a few times. Apparently, he was either the first intelligence officer with a sense of humor that I had ever encountered, or I was in for a peculiar meeting.

Michael Ross was born and raised in western Canada. Not Jewish, let alone Israeli, when he was backpacking through Europe in his early twenties, he ended up sojourning in Israel as a way to escape the cold. He met an Israeli woman, married her, converted to Judaism, and was drafted into the Israeli army. Afterward, he was recruited into Israel's famed Mossad intelligence service— and proceeded to work as an undercover operative in some of the most dangerous circumstances imaginable.

But now all that was behind him, and he was back in North America. We had been corresponding for some time, and I was looking forward to meeting him in person and asking him for his take on my project. I would be off to DC soon for my very last push at Middle East peace, and I wondered if he had any advice for me before I went.

Unfortunately, though, at the last minute I came down sick and had to cancel our meeting. I would have to settle for speaking to him on the phone, which was a little disappointing because I was curious to see if he had been serious about how I would be able to recognize him at the hotel. I mean, was he *really* going to be carrying a *Time* magazine?

"With each successive year, the knowledge base on the history of the conflict gets worse," Ross told me when I asked for his thoughts on the situation. "With every new class of Middle East experts, there is less and less grasp of the reality."

Ross explained that he thought that people studied, analyzed, and reported on the situation so much that the result was a load of often-contradictory information that was growing increasingly academic and less rooted in what was actually happening on the ground. The more the facts about Israeli military maneuvers or Hamas ideology were repeated and regurgitated by people who knew little about them, for example, the more it all became part of an unconstructive echo chamber.

"It's so obsessively and compulsively covered that it gets ridiculous," he said. "The sheer volume is just overwhelming, and so I don't blame people for being ignorant. And it's so incredibly politicized that if journalists know anything before even getting on the bloody plane, it's the wrong thing."

"So you don't see many positive contributions being made by all the pundits here?" I asked.

"I don't see any positive contribution here," he said. "There are five thousand conferences about it—and it all becomes muddled. A joke."

In his time in the Mossad, Ross had been involved in all manner of high stakes and dangerous secret exploits, from racing down European highways with explosive-laden cars to going undercover in Iran to investigate the Islamic Republic's nuclear program.

Had any of this given him a sense of hope for those people trying to foster peace?

"I've seen it close up," he said, "and it's an exercise in futility."

"Do you have any optimism at all?" I asked. "Or is it total pessimism?"

"Pessimism," he answered without any hesitation, "because the two sides will never be able to stop posing for the camera and trying to play the diplomatic propaganda game. We can never have a real discussion, because there's just way too much interference."

"Interference from whom?"

"Well, academics love this conflict," he said, "and the media thinks it's the greatest thing since sliced bread. And even the diplomats love to work on this issue. If you work on something more bland, what are you going to brag about to the girl at the local party? This is a sexy thing. You have a better chance of getting laid with it."

To be honest, this was not the first time I had heard this observation: that real progress in resolving the conflict would likely cause the people who spend their lives working on it to lose their jobs.

After a while, I started telling Ross about some of the specifics of what I'd been up to. Yossi Beilin, AIPAC, Samar Assad, the comedian Ray Hanania, the JDL, and the ISM. When I got to the ISM, Ross broke in with some things he wanted to tell me about them.

"They go through a whole training and indoctrination program," he said. "They learn what they should say at the border. How they should interact with the Israeli army. The spycraft secrets that you'd provide to someone doing dirty work in another person's country—for example, how to conceal one's identity or lie to law enforcement. They're tied to groups like Islamic Jihad, and directly involved in assisting them—providing shelter, et cetera."

I didn't know if this was true, but again I wished that the people at the ISM had been willing to be more open with me. There were a lot of bad things going on on both sides of the conflict, but there were also so many ad hominem attacks and personal aspersions flung about. I was nearing the end of my journey, about to head to DC for one final hurrah, and I was still not really any closer to knowing what was true and what was not.

I paused, frustrated once more.

"I've spoken to politicians, diplomats, academics, journalists, lobbyists, pundits, and the public," I said to him, "but I still don't have my answer. So tell me: how should I personally make peace?"

"Greg," he answered. "If I were you, I'd throw my hands above my head and say, 'This is a huge waste of my time,' and go back and enjoy life, because life is too short for dealing with all these shitheads."

Michael Ross's last words to me echoing in my head, I went off to DC, prepared to do precisely the opposite of what he had said— just one more time.

Abby's sister Melissa lived in Virginia, just outside DC, and I based myself at her house, as I often did when I visited the capital. By this point, her two sons seemed to have more or less forgotten about the recent presidential election, but there were still some obvious political threads running through the household.

Just before I arrived, for example, the younger kid, who had recently turned three, had somehow learned that Virginia—his state—had been on the losing side of the Civil War. This did not please him at all.

"No!" he shouted at his mother. "I don't want Virginia to lose!"

"Jonah," she said, "that was a long time ago, and even though Virginia lost, *our* side won."

"It's not fair!" he shrieked, starting to bubble into real tears. "I don't want Virginia to lose!"

"What we believe in *won*," his mother said again.

But it was no use. The kid was distraught about the results of the Civil War. And even if that didn't jibe at all with his recent support of Obama—and even if he was a Jewish kid who lived in *northern* Virginia and whose family was mostly from New York and Maryland—there was no way to console him.

It made me think of the Middle East conflict, some of the players in it, and a fundamental problem we all faced: too often, emotional gut responses can't be beaten by logic.

The first item on my DC agenda promised to be a bit uncomfortable. I was going to be going undercover as an Evangelical Christian.

Ever since I had seen Pastor John Hagee speak at the AIPAC conference, I had been weirdly fascinated by the movement that he led. Wildly supportive of Israel, their sensibilities and motivations would still have been foreign to any Israeli who encountered them. And the unrelentingly hawkish views that they held would have repelled any Palestinian who did. But their single-minded devotion and their jarring religious fanaticism were intriguing— and because of the sway they had on American policy, it was important.

As luck would have it, I was in DC during the annual convention of Christians United for Israel, the organization that Hagee had founded. Its membership included a couple hundred thousand Evangelical Christians, among whose primary concerns was

Israel's role in the End Times. Their conference was undoubtedly going to be an eye-opening experience.

But there was one problem. When I had contacted CUFI's media relations people about getting a press pass to the event, they had sounded noncommittal about granting one to me. I followed up a bit later, and was given a firm no.

So what I had decided to do was to forget the idea of going as a reporter, and just sign up as a regular participant—an Evangelical. Sure, I looked more Jewish than Moses, but who would know that I hadn't quite accepted Christ as my lord and savior?

This way I'd get the full experience of the conference, and maybe come to understand the relationship between Evangelicals and Israel from the inside. Maybe I'd even have a change of heart when it came to my heathen ways.

The first night of the conference was devoted to a musical prayer session.

I got there a bit early and signed in. Along with some schedules, brochures, and other material, I was given a CUFI tote bag, adorned with the slogan "For Zion's Sake I Will Not Keep Silent." It would go nicely with my PeaceMaker boxer shorts and my Jewish Defense League T-shirt, I thought. Even if I was not making peace, I was at least successfully building a whole new wardrobe.

Carrying the bag, I went to the main hall and found a seat near the back. Soon the place began to fill up, and a girl in her early twenties sat beside me. On her other side was a teenage boy who had come in with her.

She smiled at me and I gave her a quick smile in return. I wasn't sure if I was imagining it or not, but she looked confused. I definitely didn't look like the rest of the people in the hall, and I wondered if she could tell that I was a little different. Perhaps the politically correct term was "religiously challenged."

In fact, as more and more people poured in, walking down the aisle beside me or sitting nearby, I was conscious of more than a few quizzical stares. All of it could have been my imagination, of course, but I wasn't sure. Was I noticeably out of place?

"This is great, huh?" the girl beside me said to me.

"Yes," I said. "Really great."

She introduced herself as Meredith and told me that the teen-age kid with her was her younger brother. They had come from Kentucky to attend the conference.

"I'm Joey Shmeltz," I told her, using the random alias I had employed a few times back when I worked for the Israeli government.

Damn, I thought, *Even my pseudonym sounds Jewish.*

"Are you here all alone?" Meredith asked me.

I nodded.

"Well, we'll walk with you," she said.

Walk with me? I thought. *Where are we going to walk?*

Meredith was smiling at me again, and I looked at her kid brother, who was nodding, but didn't seem as enthusiastic about "walking" with me.

Before long, the evening's program got under way. Someone from CUFI welcomed the crowd and then asked for a "cheer for the Lord," which they happily provided. I clapped along, smiling at Meredith as she yelled out, "Amen! Amen!"

Then a rock band called Sonicflood took the stage and their front man told us, "Our desire is to lift up the name of Jesus Christ everywhere we go."

When they started playing, their music was actually pretty good—as long as I didn't listen too closely to the slightly disturbing lyrics.

"Pray for their welfare," they said. "Pray for their peace. Pray they will come to know Jesus, the Messiah."

When they played a lively song called "Lord of the Dance," the room seemed to morph into a full-out rock concert, and people started dancing in the same silly, improvisational manner as I'd seen arm-waving Grateful Dead fans use.

I knew that religious people were often deeply involved with their communities and causes, but although I could have understood this crowd gathering together from all over the country because of their church and their religion, it felt weird to me that they were all here dancing around for Israel, the Jewish state.

Pondering this, it took me a moment to realize that Meredith was talking to me.

"You have to dance," she said. "You can't feel the power if you don't dance."

I looked at her blankly. I wasn't entirely sure that I wanted to feel "the power," but I was one hundred percent positive that I didn't want to dance.

Up to now, as everyone gyrated around wildly and the band

jammed like they were at Woodstock, I had just been sitting there and marveling at the scene, with my arms crossed. Meredith and her brother, by contrast, had been dancing around with their arms spread wide and waving wildly above their heads. A lot of people in the room were in this same posture, which seemed to symbolize receptivity to the heavens.

"You have to dance," Meredith said again. "Dance with me! Feel the Christ!"

Now here's the thing: I can't think of very much that I hate more than dancing. In fact, this is often a bone of contention between Abby and me, because she gets irritated at my complete reluctance to set foot on a dance floor. When our wedding had been approaching, she and I had practiced what was supposed to be our first dance, and I had been dreading the moment we would do it in front of our gathered guests. But a few days before the wedding, Abby tripped and got fairly severe whiplash. This meant that our dance was not going to happen. I felt bad for my young bride, who had to wear a neck brace on her wedding day, but I was still pretty thrilled that I didn't have to dance.

And when, at the beginning of the wedding celebration, everyone did the hora, a festive Jewish group dance during which the bride and groom often are lifted up on chairs by the guests, I darted out of the room to avoid being pulled into it. Abby, neck injury and all, was hoisted into the air alone, while I went out to the bar area and had a shot of tequila with Luke.

But now, at the CUFI conference, Meredith was staring at me expectantly.

"Come on," she said. "Join us in dance."

And what I heard was "Dance, Jew, Dance!"

What was I going to do? I figured that since I was undercover and trying to have the full experience, I might as well bite the bullet and do it. And what were the odds that someone here would know me and see me dancing around? I might even have a spiritual awakening. So I danced along with Meredith and her brother, and with all the other Evangelicals surrounding me.

And as I danced to Sonicflood, I put my arms up in that weird receptive-to-the-heavens pose most of the others had when they danced. Meanwhile, the lights swirled around us, the crowd screamed in ecstasy, and the musicians onstage rocked out.

"That's it!" Meredith exclaimed, clapping her hands. "That's it!"

Look at this, I thought. *I'm actually part of something.*

And while I waited for a spiritual revelation to overcome me—one that would not only solve any existential problems I had, but also help me make peace while simultaneously eradicating my distaste for dancing—I thought about what I might tell Abby if she found out about this episode.

"It's nothing personal," I decided I would tell her. "Only Jesus can make me dance."

The rest of the CUFI conference sort of felt like a surreal version of what I had experienced at AIPAC. Everyone was as single-minded and hawkish as they had been at AIPAC, but the addition of apocalyptic religious zeal made it that much zanier.

For example, before many of the panel and speaking sessions, the moderator would ask the crowd to join him in a prayer, and all of us would bow our heads in unison. And many times I heard people matter-of-factly intertwining theology and American national interests so completely that it was clear that in their minds they really were one and the same.

I ran into Meredith occasionally during the conference, and found out a bit more about her. She was a college student who had been raised Evangelical but had only somewhat recently become focused on the Middle East.

"What makes you so interested in it?" I asked, as we waited for one of the panel discussions to begin.

She shrugged, then said, "Well, if it wasn't in the Bible, I wouldn't care. But I'm a Christian, and I'm pretty hard-core about that."

I've noticed, I wanted to say, but bit my tongue.

"And when it comes to Israel," she continued, "we need more people to step up to the plate."

Needless to say, Meredith fit right in at the conference.

"Neither the land of Israel nor the Jews," one speaker told the crowd, "makes sense without God. And he says that if you let my people live in my land, you have no idea how good it's going to be for you."

At this, of course, there was tremendous applause.

Loads of speakers spouted CUFI's bread and butter doctrines of an imminent End Time brought about by the ingathering of the Jews in Israel. The believers would be pitted against the heathens, final battles would be waged, and rivers of blood would engulf a flaming apocalyptic landscape. But mixed in with all the fundamentalist Christian speakers, there were also a couple of rabbis who looked even more out of place than I did, except that they had clearly made common cause with the CUFI crowd as invited speakers at various sessions during the conference.

"There are no political solutions for a theological conflict," one of them told us from the podium.

Again there were cheers from the crowd, but this line was particularly jarring to me. I don't have very fond feelings toward religion, and the more it involved itself in the conflict, the less confident I was that *anyone* could make peace in the Middle East. I remembered a high-ranking Israeli government strategist once telling me that whenever he was involved with articulating the Israeli position, he was always careful to couch it in political terms.

"The more it becomes seen as a religious conflict," he had told me, "the less chance we have of ever getting anywhere."

But these people seemed able only to see it in religious terms. Kind of like Islamic Jihad did.

Which is why, when former presidential candidate Gary Bauer, who spoke later in the conference, brought up militant Islam, I thought he might be missing the mark.

"You are Hamas's and Hezbollah's—and probably our own State Department's—worst nightmare," he said, meaning that it was the membership of CUFI that would ensure that American support stayed unblinkingly behind even the most hawkish of Israeli policies.

"There is nothing that diplomats will be able to accomplish," Bauer continued, "that is not first accomplished on the battlefield."

I wasn't sure, though, that I agreed that these people were really Hamas's and Hezbollah's worst nightmare. Sometimes it seemed like there was a de facto alliance between those on either side who seemed to want perpetual war, or an apocalyptic struggle between religions.

Bauer went on to say that with Barack Obama, the "chain" of presidents who instinctively understood the bond America had with Israel had been "broken."

At this point, someone in the back of the room screamed out, "I disagree!"

This caused a wave of angry mumbling to roll over the crowd.

"Well, you can go disagree somewhere else, my friend!" Bauer proclaimed, and the room erupted into wild applause.

Later, Rick Santorum, the former U.S. senator, told the throngs of adoring Christians that in the American-Israeli relationship, these were "desperate times."

"Yes!" an old woman in the crowd yelled. "Yes!"

"There is no foreign policy taught in Chicago," he went on. "Obama was taught where he's from . . . the world."

I wasn't totally sure what he meant by this last statement. The best case, I figured, was that he was suggesting that the president was cosmopolitan and worldly in a way that did not appeal to a staunchly conservative Christian audience. He could have also meant, though, that Obama was an outsider, a foreigner— simply not a real American.

"Yes!" the old woman shrieked, seemingly on the verge of collapsing from enthusiasm. "Yes!"

When CUFI's grassroots soldiers went up to Capitol Hill to

talk to their representatives, Santorum said, "You have to strike the fear of God in them!"

"Yes!" the woman continued on. "Yes! Yes!"

I was not entirely sure she was even listening.

Later, to endless applause, David Brog, CUFI's executive director, gave the attendees some information about the organization. There were over 230,000 Christians involved with it, he said. And since that was far bigger than AIPAC in terms of numbers, that made CUFI the "largest Zionist organization in the world."

"But with fifty million Evangelicals, and many more Christians," he went on, "that's barely a start."

I looked at Meredith, who was sitting with me at the time. Her eyes were glued to Brog, and she was nodding with every word he said.

In essence, Brog, Hagee, and their followers were trying to grow stronger and more influential in order to push American policies to become increasingly hawkish in the Middle East— and more and more supportive of the extreme Right-wingers in Israel. As farfetched as it may have seemed to an outsider like me, the end goal of this was to bring about a final battle: the Rapture, Evangelical Christianity's End Times, Armageddon. To them, politics was just an extension of religion—and the Middle East was their holy battlefield.

"We need to build this organization bigger and stronger," Brog told the crowd. "The clock is ticking."

*   *   *

After the CUFI conference, my next stop felt a whole lot more grounded, though some people I knew might have thought it was just as outlandish as CUFI, if not more. Jeremy Ben-Ami's J-Street was now fully up and running, and I was going to visit its office.

Although the young organization's fund-raising had definitely gotten rolling, its war chest was still minuscule compared to AIPAC's coffers—and its office was accordingly modest. In the front, a bunch of twenty-something staffers worked the phones, and in a back office, Jeremy Ben-Ami dealt with the high-level issues.

While I waited for him to be ready to speak to me, I sat in that outside area and watched his youthful team do their parts in trying to reshape the American relationship to the Middle East.

"We've got a lot of signatures on it," one of them was saying into the phone, "but we would really like the congressman's support."

Daniel Levy—though definitely a strong force within J-Street—continued to be based in the world of think tanks, and I figured this was a decision based on him not being an American citizen. If J-Street was going to change DC's Middle East power dynamics, it had to be careful about how it presented itself.

In fact, as it had begun to get more and more momentum, it had started to attract a lot more attention, both negative and positive, and debates were beginning to swirl around it with increasing intensity. Predictably, Right-wingers in the United States and Israel were labeling it anti-Israel, but it was also getting only a lukewarm welcome by some Centrists who seemed unsure what to make of it.

A fair number of congressmen and senators had signed onto

J-Street's proposals and initiatives, and the body language of the White House made quite plain that they were on the same page as the organization. Recently, in fact, the president had met with a select group of representatives from the Jewish world to discuss his approach to the Middle East. At the meeting, he had told the assembled leaders that he intended to engage with the conflict in a hands-on manner and push forcefully for a two-state solution and a regional peace effort, which was essentially what J-Street had been founded to foster. J-Street, new on the scene, had been in the room, a fact that had reportedly irked some of the more established organizations.

That was something I wanted to ask Kevin about—if he and I ever actually managed to connect.

J-Street had also announced that it would be holding its first conference, presumably modeled after AIPAC's annual event. And an interesting issue on the table was the question of how successful it would be. How many congressmen and senators would attend? Who would provide their support? And perhaps most intriguingly, how would Israel's hawkish government respond?

Would the Israeli ambassador be there?

That, I thought, would be a significant sign about the way Israel would view this new dovish force in DC politics.

Was the organization tenable in the long term?

While I waited for Ben-Ami, I checked my phone to see if the Israeli Embassy had responded to my requests for a meeting. The Palestinian Mission had eventually responded positively to my faxed request, and I had a meeting set up with them for the end of the week. But I still hadn't heard back from the Israelis.

All I had was a text message from Luke, who wanted to know if I was going to the "flower-themed party" Jacob had invited us all to. I still didn't really know what that was all about and didn't have time to figure it out now, because one of Ben-Ami's assistants told me that her boss was ready to see me.

I went into his office and sat down across from him. Behind me, I noticed, there was a dry-erase board with a list of lawmakers who were supporting a particular J-Street initiative.

"So how's it going?" I asked. "How is J-Street working out?"

"Pretty good," Ben-Ami said. "We now have a hundred and ten thousand people on the email list, have doubled the budget to three million, and have doubled the staff—all this in hard economic times."

"And what do you attribute these successes to?"

"Well," he said, "we're showing that a vacuum exists. There has been a complete absence of a voice with rational, progressive values that cares about Israel—but also wants justice for the Palestinians. And we're doing something concrete. We're helping politicians understand that they'd actually be able to raise money even if they supported that kind of approach. Over the decades, a terrible fear has developed that they wouldn't be able to if they supported a serious, sustained U.S. leadership instead of a hands-off attitude."

"And where do you go from here?"

"Our focus now," he said, "is turning our political capital into policy change."

AIPAC's thinking, he went on, was that when it came to making peace, the U.S. should go with the pace taken by the Israeli government, but even one beat slower. J-Street's, he said, was to step on the accelerator.

He knew that I was in a rush to solve the conflict too, and I had told him earlier the working title of my new book, *How to Make Peace in the Middle East in Six Months or Less Without Leaving Your Apartment*. Now he paused for a second, and then referenced it.

"Six months is the right approach," he said, "there's no time to waste. The U.S. needs to be extremely active at the table. It needs to do far more than just serving coffee."

"So what should I do to make peace?" I asked. "I don't want to just serve coffee either."

"The key is to get all the players into an isolated location for as long as it takes," he said. "Shut the door and not let them go."

I nodded. Maybe this was what I needed to do all along. Kidnap influential politicians and forcibly confine them. It was just crazy enough to work.

Later I went to AIPAC's headquarters, a colossal building close to Capitol Hill. After J-Street's unassuming offices, it was a bit overpowering.

Josh Block, AIPAC's spokesperson whom I'd met at the AIPAC conference, met me downstairs and escorted me up. We passed through numerous hallways, and beside a lot of offices and cubicles, and there seemed to be dozens or even hundreds of people in the building. At one point Josh led me through a boardroom that had a long wooden table surrounded by sleek chairs. It was a big, overwhelming room, and I marveled at the fact that it actually seemed bigger—and was undoubtedly more luxuriously decorated—than the cabinet room of the Israeli government, where I had sometimes sat in on parts of meetings.

For some people, I thought, that AIPAC conference room would have seemed like the very heart of what they considered the "Israel Lobby," or in cases of outright anti-Semitism, of Jewish control of the United States government.

Eventually Block showed me to a little meeting room, and we sat down together. I explained to him more fully what I was doing, and he smiled—even though, as Samar Assad had said, if I was successful, I would put him out of business.

"What do you think of Obama's emphasis on the settlements?" I asked.

"Look," Block said, "let's just be frank, okay? AIPAC has never advocated on settlements, for or against. As an American organization, it doesn't take positions on internal Israeli matters like that. And while settlements are clearly an issue that the parties will need to address, it's not the most crucial or difficult, nor is it the impediment to peace. At the moment, that's still an unwillingness on the part of the Palestinians to engage in a serious peace process without preconditions they invent or seize to avoid making the kind of painful sacrifices Israel has proven itself willing to make for the sake of peace, as it did with Egypt and Jordan.

"In reality, there are far more important and productive things to focus on, and certainly the Obama administration's early experiences, as well intentioned as their overall approach may have been, proves that. Israel did things it has never done before—under any government, Labor, Kadima, or Likud—to restrain settlement activity, and what did we see from the Arabs and Palestinians? Backsliding and recalcitrance. Sad, really."

For Block and AIPAC, a more pressing issue at the moment was Iran.

"AIPAC is using all of its clout to halt the Iranian nuclear program," he said, "and in this, it is on the same page as a large majority of the American people, and their elected officials."

As much as the Palestinian issue often dominated the headlines in the West, he wanted to stress, "For those in America interested in Israel's survival and vitality, and America's national security interests in the region, the existential threat provided by Iran, and its relentless support of America's and Israel's terrorist enemies, is the real problem."

If Iran was neutralized, AIPAC believed, its nefarious influence—exporting arms, training, and ideology to Palestinian terrorist groups—would disappear, helping to bring regional calm.

I knew, though, that others, such as J-Street, thinkers like Samar Assad, and the Palestinians themselves, often made the opposite case. Dealing with the Palestinian-Israeli conflict once and for all would not only give Israel credibility in the eyes of the world, they believed. It would also take the issue of Palestinian suffering and disenfranchisement off the table, so that powers like Iran could not use it as an excuse for their continuing aggression.

AIPAC's stance seemed to be that Iran had to be dealt with one way or another as soon as possible, and the Palestinian-Israeli track would have to proceed at a slower pace, mostly because the Palestinian leaders were unwilling or unable to take the opportunities for peace that they were offered.

"Israel has made countless concessions," Block continued, "and the Palestinian leadership just keeps digging its heels in, and everyone suffers as a result. Our view is that we are not in a position to dictate to our ally Israel what they need for their security from thousands of miles away—they understand best what is right to protect their children from the real and genuine threats surrounding them.

"I'm an American. I don't serve in the army there, or put my kids on the bus there, or live with the consequences of the risks they take for peace. They do. And as an American who supports Israel and sees their security as critically important for them and for America's national security interests, I respect their experience and the choices they make for themselves. Otherwise, I guess, one doesn't respect their quite vibrant democracy, their place as our ally, or their right to democratic self-government."

"What do you make of the 'friends don't let friends drive drunk' argument?" I asked. "That the United States should push Israel to help itself. Say, by curtailing settlements."

This argument, in essence, was that since Israel's settlement-building, hard-line security measures, and reluctance to make concessions to the Palestinians were not in its own long-term survival interests, the best thing the United States could do, as a friend, was to pressure Israel to curtail this counterproductive behavior. Just like a friend might take away another friend's car keys if he was too drunk to drive and was liable to hurt himself and others.

"I think that's condescending," Block said. "In the case of the settlements, they are an issue, but one that is part of the negotiations between the two sides to discuss in that context.

"AIPAC wants the United States to work together with our friends in Israel on a bipartisan basis, as we do with all our closest democratic allies in the world. Advocating for that kind of special ally-to-ally relationship is what makes AIPAC's bipartisan pro-Israel approach different from those groups—on the fringe Left and Right—who think they know better than anyone, including the people of Israel, and then advocate for American public pressure and confrontation with our allies in the Jewish state as a means of achieving their own ideological aims."

When I brought up the issue of AIPAC's oft-cited power and influence, Block downplayed the hype surrounding it.

"That stems from AIPAC's unique role, lobbying the one issue that is truly bipartisan and so broadly supported by the American public," he said. "Have you ever tried pushing on an open door?

"Beyond that," he went on, "it's silly conspiracy theories about Jewish power fueled by the same marginal figures that have always been there. Look, who was more prominent in American life, Charles Lindbergh—one of the most vile and outspoken anti-Jewish conspiracists known to man—or some professor you've never heard of who says Jews and their allies have warped the minds of the American public? The fringe ten percent who see bogeymen under their bed have always been around, and they are less prevalent today than in the past.

"Could it possibly be that hundreds of millions of Americans are simply pro-Israel," he continued, "because, unlike the rest of the countries in the Middle East, Israel is the only place that respects freedom of speech and religion, and the rest of our fundamental democratic values? I think so. And poll after poll proves it."

Our time was nearly up by now, and I soon readied to head out.

"Dude," Block said, just before I left. "I hear your first book was really funny. I'll have to get a copy."

I smiled. There was no question about it now. Whether or not I agreed with every aspect of the AIPAC agenda, I definitely liked its spokesman.

I walked off, staring up once more at AIPAC's imposing headquarters. In a way, I thought, AIPAC seemed to send mixed messages, both waving off the idea that it was overly influential, and doing things—like sending out frequent press releases about its legislative successes—that highlighted its power.

I didn't think that this stemmed from some sort of confusion in branding or strategy. Rather, I thought that it might be a clever and nuanced overall messaging strategy, though I didn't pretend to fully understand it.

When later in the week I spoke to M. J. Rosenberg, the director of policy analysis for the dovish Israel Policy Forum, he told me that he thought that even AIPAC's building—huge, expensive, and imposing—served to send a message to Washington.

"AIPAC looms larger in Washington than Israel itself does," he said.

Rosenberg also told me that as J-Street gained momentum while obviously connecting to the new U.S. administration, he thought small chinks were starting to appear in AIPAC's armor and Washington's status quo attitude on the Middle East. For example, more congressmen and senators were willing to critique

Israeli policy without fear of negative blowback. Rosenberg was, unsurprisingly, excited about the promise the Obama administration offered.

"Unlike other presidents, Obama says to the Israelis in private what he says to them in public," he said.

I brought up Josh Block's comment about condescension. What did Rosenberg make of the argument that the United States telling Israel what to do was condescending?

"The U.S. provides far more aid to Israel than to anyone else," he said, "and no aid should be unconditional. If Israel doesn't like it, Israel should wean itself from American aid. But from our perspective, American interests should come first."

Oddly, some of this sounded not so different from what someone on the far other end of the spectrum had once told me. Daniel Pipes, one of the most stridently hawkish Middle East analysts around, had said to me that he opposed Israel taking American money because it distorted Israeli policies.

(Distorted them leftward, presumably. Pipes had also told me that the Obama administration was a "bunch of amateurs" who didn't realize that "you don't get what you want from the Israelis by pushing them around." And that as a historian he knew that "peace is made when one side gives up," which meant that the way to make peace in the Middle East was for a total, overwhelming and lasting defeat of one side or the other.)

"Does it ever tire you out?" I asked M. J. Rosenberg. "The constant debate?"

He nodded and said, "Well, my firm rule is that I never discuss Israel or the Middle East in social situations."

That was really good idea, I thought.

"Well, I don't want to discuss it at *all* anymore," I told him, "but in order to do that, I think I need to solve the conflict myself."

He looked at me and raised his eyebrows a bit.

"And, unfortunately, I don't have much time left anymore," I added. "So what should I do?"

"Sit down with the leaders and put forward your own plan," he said. "You should use person to person contact, because you're a very charming person, with a North American innocence about you. And you have adorable hair."

Over the next few days, adorable hair and all, I ran around DC, meeting with various other pundits, journalists, bloggers, and activists to see if anyone could tell me anything substantively new, and finding out that they pretty much couldn't. But it was what I had scheduled for my last day in the capital that I was most interested in.

That last day I had back-to-back appointments that promised to offer quite a contrast to each other. The first was with Nabil Abuznaid, the head of the Palestinian Mission to the United States and a former advisor to Yasser Arafat.

The second was with Meyrav Wurmser, an Israeli American who was a close personal friend and sometime advisor to high-ranking members of the new right-wing government in Israel, including the prime minister, Benjamin Netanyahu.

Even though I had made repeated calls and sent emails to the

Israeli Embassy, I had never heard back from them. I'd contacted a friend who had worked in the Israeli prime minister's office with me, and he'd connected me to someone in the embassy, but this still had not yielded any results. Even when I left messages about how I was writing an article for *Newsweek*—more on that shortly—I had received no response. I hadn't used my last name, so it wasn't as if this were because of a personal problem with me. I guess they were just too busy to make peace.

But I figured that Meyrav Wurmser, with her tight connections to the people in the prime minister's office in Jerusalem, would serve as an ideal proxy.

In fact, this last day of my trip was as close as I was going to come to actually bringing the Israelis and Palestinians together in any meaningful sense. When I had started this endeavor, I had harbored vague fantasies of getting senior officials from both sides into a room and hashing out an agreement once and for all. But it seemed that these back-to-back meetings were as good as I was going to get.

One thing that had crossed my mind, though, had been the idea of just scheduling both meetings at the same time and place.

"Meet me at Starbucks at eleven," I'd say to both of them, and then when they both showed up at the same time, we'd have a little laugh about the mix-up and then they'd sit down and make peace over butterscotch blondies and iced coffees. Or possibly just try to stab each other in the face with Starbucks spoons.

In any case, as I saw it, this morning represented the high point of my peacemaking activities. I was going to try to find common ground between them. If I could just facilitate even a partial meeting of the minds, maybe it would be enough of a foundation to build something on. I could shuttle between the two offices, and then when we'd nailed down the basic skeleton for our peace plan, Abuznaid would send word to his superiors in Ramallah, and Wurmser would call up her friends in Jerusalem. Then I'd call Kevin, my contact in the Obama administration and bring him up to speed. Soon we'd all be on the White House grounds, shaking hands for the cameras.

Today was the day. And I knew that it called for an extra bit of luck. So, when I got dressed and got ready to go, I finally put on my PeaceMaker boxer shorts.

Before I left her house that morning, Abby's sister Melissa decided to tell her kids what I was up to.

"Do you know what Uncle Greg is going to do today?" she began. "He's going to try to make peace. Do you know what that means?"

The two boys, who were immersed in eating string cheese, didn't respond. I took this to mean that while they knew about war—or, for some reason, at least the Civil War—they had apparently never heard of peace.

"It means," their mom went on, "that he's trying to stop people from fighting. Do you have any ideas for him about how to do that?"

Jonah didn't answer. He was too busy chewing a disproportionately large piece of cheese. But Ben put down his cheese for a moment and suddenly looked thoughtful.

"They shouldn't be mean," he said. "And, and, and—"

He was getting out of breath, trying to sputter out the rest of his diplomacy lesson.

"And," he continued, "and, and, and, if they are mean, and they fight, you should give them a time-out."

He picked up his string cheese again and began chewing it, and he and his little brother both looked at me for approval.

"Yeah," Jonah added, nodding.

I smiled and thanked them for their advice, wondering if maybe it might actually be useful.

I'd walk into the Palestinian Mission, sit in front of Nabil Abuznaid, and say, "It's just time to stop being so mean."

Or I'd go into Meyrav Wurmser's office and say, "If you guys don't stop fighting, I'm going to have to separate you."

When I'd been in touch with the Palestinian Mission to arrange the meeting, I'd reflexively expected them to ask for my passport details so that they could check up on me for security reasons. That, of course, had been a part of every interaction I'd had with Israeli officials, and most I'd had with Americans.

But no. All I had to do, they said, was show up. And then "Peter would take care of everything."

I had no idea who Peter was, but I was glad that he was on the job, and also a little pleased that they didn't seem to care about checking up on me. I didn't have anything to hide, really, but I wasn't sure what they'd think if they realized I had once worked for the Israelis.

So I just showed up at the address the Mission had given me, a relatively nondescript building near Dupont Circle, and went upstairs.

And, sure enough, Peter was up there waiting. He didn't look Palestinian, I noticed, but East Asian instead. As I waited to be shown in to meet Abuznaid, I wandered around the foyer a little. It was quite amazing, not just in its austerity, but also in the way it seemed to be so temporary. Furniture and artwork were just sort of haphazardly placed around the room, and there were files stacked up chaotically, as if the Mission was preparing to move. The only item that seemed intentionally positioned was a three-dimensional model of Jerusalem sitting on a table by the entrance.

I had seen similar models in Israeli offices, actually, and I couldn't really see much of a difference in this one. The troubled city looked the same, with no readily discernible signs of politics.

When Peter led me into Dr. Nabil Abuznaid's office, I found two suited middle-aged Palestinian men there, standing up and talking. I assumed the one standing behind the desk was Abuznaid, but had no idea who the other one was.

"Hi," the one I didn't know said, putting out his hand for me to shake.

"Hi. I'm Gregory Levey," I told him, grasping his hand and waiting for him to tell me who he was, or at least give me his name. He didn't, and seemed to be waiting for me to give him more info about myself instead.

It's a long story, I thought, and just stood there looking at him.

After a few moments of this—which felt a little awkward—he just nodded and left the room.

Almost immediately, it became clear that Abuznaid actually didn't have much more information about what I was doing there than his colleague did. In fact, he seemed pretty unclear on how this meeting had been arranged or what I was doing in his office.

"So . . ." he said, sitting down and indicating for me to do the same. "Why are you here?"

I explained the situation as best as I could and, with little more than a shrug, he accepted the idea that I was there to make peace. Essentially, he didn't seem to particularly care and gave off the impression that people came into his office trying to make peace all the time—which was probably the case.

"So . . ." I began uncertainly. "What was Chairman Arafat like?"

"He was very nice," Abuznaid said with another shrug.

Needless to say, that wasn't exactly what I'd heard. But as we spoke, Dr. Abuznaid himself did really seem very nice. He was warm and welcoming and very generous with his time, and he seemed a lot more grounded than many of the Middle East debaters native to the United States.

In fact, he himself was aware of this irony:

"Sometimes people here sound more radical than people there," he said. "It's often easier to talk to the Israelis."

He told me that although it was still too early to tell, he thought the messages and moves emerging from the new White House were encouraging. It was heartening, he explained, that Obama spoke about the rights and the suffering of both sides.

"The problem," he said, "is that people have to see actions. So Obama will have to either lose credibility or have a serious confrontation with the Israelis. We have heard lots of talk before, and we want to see actions. Palestinians want schools, education, hospitals. They want a better life."

Abuznaid paused, and pursed his lips.

Then he said, "You need to tell Americans that what happened to the Jews and the Palestinians is that we were both victims of history. What happened in Europe was not done by Palestinians and Muslims. It happened in the heart of Christianity in Europe, and it is not an excuse for what the Israelis do to us now."

I thought of my uncle, and of the JDL's mantra of "Never Again."

Generally, Abuznaid was calm and friendly during our talk, but I did get him worked up twice. The first time was when I asked about the Israeli disengagement from the Gaza Strip—which had been orchestrated by Ariel Sharon, while I had been working for the Israeli government.

"The Israelis never left Gaza," he told me. "They control the air, the water, and the land. And the conditions in Gaza are terrible. The poverty. People are dying. I agree that the rocket attacks against Israel from Gaza should stop, but people have to understand the situation in Gaza too."

Abuznaid was clearly getting upset. He spoke fairly calmly, but I could see a barely concealed simmering anger.

"When Sharon left unilaterally," he continued, "he made a mistake. He never worked with the Palestinian Authority to allow it to get credit for it from the people. That allowed Hamas to get the credit."

What I did next was try to conduct some shuttle diplomacy. I was heading to see Prime Minister Netanyahu's friend and sometime advisor next, I told him. What did he want me to tell her? What did he want me to tell the Israelis?

"Tell them this," he said. "If they don't get peace now, when are they going to get it? Why do they think things will always stay in their favor? Say to them that if the Israeli fear today is coming from a distance away—from Tehran—why do they fear the Palestinians? Tell the Israelis that if we get a state, you will get relations with fifty-seven other countries. Tell them that today the Israelis are the ones never missing opportunities to miss opportunities. Tell them that there is momentum today, and they should not ignore it. The ball is in their court."

But besides all that, Abuznaid also had something personal to say. Why, he wanted to know, couldn't he take his family to visit Jerusalem? In a few weeks, he told me, he would be taking his children—one was fourteen and the other was twenty-three—to visit their homeland. While they were in the West Bank, he said, he really wanted to take them to see Jerusalem. By this point they were all American citizens, he said, but even so, they would not be allowed in.

"Really?" I asked. "Even though you're all American?"

He nodded.

"Here in Washington," he said, "I meet with the Israeli ambassador at the best restaurant in town, and we enjoy lunch together. There, the Israelis would stop me from taking my kids to see the holy sites in Jerusalem."

This definitely didn't seem right to me, and I couldn't believe it was true. This was the case even for Palestinians who were also American citizens?

"Really?" I asked, still skeptical.

"I challenge any Israeli to prove me wrong about this restriction," he said. "I'll be there on the twentieth of the month. Under any condition, can I go to Jerusalem?"

Abuznaid seemed understandably disgusted by this. But he also seemed a little disgusted by his situation in DC. The Palestinian Mission in Washington, he told me, had to report all their activities to the State Department every six months in order to maintain their status. Worse, because of all the lawsuits against them, the Mission was not even able to have a bank account, or checks. All their expenses for office work and the day-to-day operations of the Mission, he said, all the way down to pencils and paper, had to be paid for privately by its employees, who were later reimbursed.

"How can you run a place like this?" he asked, waving a hand in front of his face, as if he were eager to brush it all away.

And, in fact, he was. After his trip to the Middle East with his kids, he would not be returning to the diplomatic pressure cooker in DC. He was going to be moving to Amsterdam instead.

"Are you happy to be going there?" I asked him.

"Very," he said, and smiled.

* * *

"I've just come from the Palestinian Mission," I told Meyrav Wurmser when I arrived in her office. I still thought that maybe I could do some shuttle diplomacy between her and Abuznaid.

"Lovely," she said, and the sarcasm in her voice told me that maybe that wasn't going to be so easy.

Wurmser said that she had recently been spending a lot of time in Israel, talking to "top people" about where things might be heading in the region—and the prevailing attitude was wholly pessimistic. I knew that the prime minister was a friend of hers and that she had previously drafted policy recommendations for him, but she told me that Israel's current national security advisor, Uzi Arad, was "like family" to her.

"So what's your current thinking on peacemaking?" I asked.

"I'm tired of it," she said. "I got to the point of burnout. This is a puzzle I can't figure out a way to solve. Especially after Hamas took over."

"So what do you think of this White House's progress and plans?"

"I think that by the time the Obama crowd catches up and catches on, they'll be in trouble up to their necks," she said. "But they need to go through their own failures with the Arab-Israeli conflict, and realize some things. One: they can't solve it. And two: it's not that important anymore."

"What do you mean?" I asked. "Not that important anymore?"

"I think we're at the end of the Arab world," she shrugged. "With Iranian domination of the region, we may have reached the end of Arabism."

This was obviously an enormous statement, but it was not the first time I had heard it. Iranian dominance, some analysts believed, was growing to such an extent in the region—following the overthrow of Iraq and the growing power of Iran-backed Hezbollah—that it was completely overwhelming the power of the Arab states, even with their shared identities and interests, their "Arabism."

Not sure where to go from there, I brought up some of the things Nabil Abuznaid had said to me and mentioned his challenge, explaining that he couldn't take his children to visit Jerusalem.

Wurmser nodded and said, "That really is unfortunate."

"What should I tell the Palestinians?" I asked her.

Wurmser rolled her eyes.

"I'd tell them that it's time to have an honest discussion about Palestinian nationalism. It was an experiment that got a lot of support—far more than the early Zionists did—but it has failed miserably. Why? Why is their story so devastatingly bad? Certainly there are settlers that burn their fields and all that, but come on. These guys had their chance."

It didn't seem like there was much possibility of a substantive meeting of the minds between Wurmser and Abuznaid. In fact, if there was any common ground between them at all, it was precisely in the hopelessness of peacemaking, in the dismal odds of there ever being any successes and the feeling that the thing to do was just to throw up one's hands and give up.

Indeed, when I asked Wurmser directly what I should personally do to help bring about peace, she shook her head as if to brush it all away, and said, "The dream of peace is only a temptress."

With All Due Respect, You Must Be on Crack

*   *   *

Being publicly called the "stupidest man on earth" is not the type of thing you brag about, even if it is by a former deputy assistant secretary of the U.S. Treasury. Still, it feels like a bit of an accomplishment. I wasn't the tallest man on earth, and I wasn't the richest man on earth. But maybe I was the stupidest man on earth. At least, I thought, it was a superlative people from my high school might be jealous of at our next reunion.

After my meetings with Abuznaid and Wurmser, here's how I got the label.

One day, just before I had closed in on this final push to make peace, an editor I knew at *Newsweek* had contacted me with a proposition.

Would I be interested in writing a Middle East opinion piece for them? he wanted to know. In particular, would I be interested in arguing something more than a little controversial?

It sounded crazy to me when he first suggested it—and still sounds crazy to me—but his idea was that I would argue that President Obama should make George W. Bush his Middle East envoy.

It was hard to think of anyone who would consider this a good idea. Obama would never want to squander all the goodwill with which he was beginning his term. Bush would never want to be anyone's messenger. And the Palestinians and the rest of the Arabs would hardly be amenable to anything that Bush brought to the table after he had spent eight years angering them.

But the idea behind this *Newsweek* piece was not to literally

233

suggest that Obama send Bush. It was to shake things up a bit and implicitly suggest that a diplomatic middle ground needed to be found, whereby Israel would still trust the United States even as the White House pushed for ambitious moves toward peace. For me, it would also serve as a sort of culmination of my final trip to DC, a place to try to assimilate all I had learned into one—obviously bad—plan.

And so I agreed, and wrote the piece up. Among other things, it said:

> During the Bush years, Israelis were consistently among the few foreign populations that gave the American president high approval marks—often in far greater proportion than Americans themselves. Senior officials in the Israeli Prime Minister's Office, where I worked, spoke on their cell phones daily with their White House counterparts—circumventing the State Department and the Israeli Foreign Ministry entirely.
>
> That closeness paid off. It's no coincidence that, during the Bush years, Ariel Sharon had political cover to suggest "painful concessions" for peace—a euphemism for withdrawal from territory. The unilateral withdrawal from the Gaza Strip—followed by preparations to withdraw from large parts of the West Bank that were interrupted only by the Hizbullah war of 2006—almost certainly would not have happened with anyone else in the White House less trusted to ensure Israel's safety.

Basically, all I was suggesting was that in order for Israel to make the concessions necessary for peace, the moves that would please people like Nabil Abuznaid, Israelis like Meyrav Wurmser would first have to trust the Obama White House in the same way that they had trusted the Bush one.

Before long, *Newsweek* ran the article. And then all hell broke loose.

It seemed to me that if you actually read my article all the way through and had at least some degree of ability in reading comprehension, it was pretty damn clear that it wasn't meant to be taken literally. Were none of these people reading the whole article before responding to it? Was the Middle East such a hot potato that people came out shooting at any new idea at all before even really considering what it represented?

The *Newsweek* website was flooded with comments, most of them angry, about what I had written, and I suddenly got more than my usual daily share of heated emails. Most of them were from a whole new wave of ranting cranks, but I also got emails from some of the connected and consequential people I had encountered over the past few months. Rather than disapproving, they just seemed amused and baffled by my modest proposal.

J-Street's Daniel Levy, for example, wrote me, "I see you're getting some serious play for your op-ed. Not necessarily all positive but it certainly attracted attention!"

But besides the emails, the piece got attacked and lampooned in what seemed like an endless number of websites and publications, including *The Atlantic, The American Prospect,* and *The New*

Republic. And on his website, a former deputy assistant secretary of the U.S. Treasury under Bill Clinton labeled me the "Stupidest Man on Earth."

For the next two days or so, it seemed like every minute I would get a new irate response, find a new article criticizing me, or receive a new angry email or phone call. This went on and on, until friends and family started contacting me to see if I was holding up okay under the barrage of pushback. And while I had expected the anger to die down after a while, it actually seemed like the responses just got more and more bitter.

Toward the end of all this, I received my favorite one, from some random internet citizen.

"With all due respect, Mr. Levey," he wrote to me, "you must be on crack."

Was this all I had to show for all my months of trying to solve the conflict? For my discussions with Nabil Abuznaid, Meyrav Wurmser, and all the rest?

Had it all been just so that I could be called the stupidest man on earth, and accused of being on crack?

CHAPTER TWELVE

Making Peace

When I left DC, I was a little worn out by the experience. There had been too many voices and too many opinions for me to sort it all out. Echoing in my mind were the words of AIPAC, of J-Street, of Nabil Abuznaid, and of Meyrav Wurmser. But also of the Evangelical preachers at the CUFI conference and the letter writer who had accused me of being on crack—and of my little nephews saying that everyone involved should just be given a time-out. It was me, I thought, that needed a time-out.

I hadn't made peace. That was for sure, but I at least wanted to believe that I had done *something*. But before I settled back at my apartment to figure it all out, there was one more thing I had to do.

Jacob was now visiting New York, and he had been invited to a bizarre event—the "flower party" he'd mentioned earlier in that email—and been given permission to bring along a few friends. A man called "Sir Ivan," who was apparently some kind of eccentric billionaire, was holding a flower-themed party called

Castlestock at his "castle" in the Hamptons. It cost five hundred dollars to attend, with all the money going to Sir Ivan's "Peaceman Foundation," but our admission would be complimentary because of Jacob's well-connected friend. When he explained it to me, my immediate thought was, *No way in hell am I going to that.* But as I considered it a bit more, I realized that I couldn't really say no, given my project. It was just too perfect.

The idea of going to any flamboyant party in the Hamptons didn't appeal to me at all, let alone one put on in a castle by someone named Sir Ivan. But the fact was that the party revolved around the concept of peace and peacemaking—Sir Ivan's other moniker was "the Peaceman"—so how could I turn it down? And when I read a bit more about Sir Ivan, it became clear that no matter how odd he sounded, his life story and his instincts were somewhat related to my own project.

Sir Ivan's father, Siegbert Wilzig, was a Holocaust survivor who had made it through two concentration camps. Fifty-nine members of his family had been murdered by the Nazis. After reaching the United States with nothing, he had gone into banking, amassing a huge fortune—despite, or perhaps because of, reportedly suffering from severe post-traumatic stress disorder. His son Ivan had initially worked in his father's bank, but had eventually quit to pursue his interest in music. Specializing in techno remixes, he had managed to have some success of his own.

And with the family fortune, he had started the Peaceman Foundation. It was a little unclear to me what his foundation did, but its literature suggested that it worked to help American soldiers suffering from post-traumatic stress disorder and to generally foster peace. He had been inspired to do this, I read, by the events of September 11, and by Palestinian suicide bombings against Israel in the Second Intifada.

And that's how Sir Ivan became known as the Peaceman—a title I coveted.

I warily accepted Jacob's invitation, and Abby and I met Jacob, his wife Nicole, his sister Zvia, and Luke at Bryant Park in midtown Manhattan. Sir Ivan had arranged for four or five buses to take his party guests from there out to his castle.

We boarded one of the buses, along with a couple dozen other confused-looking guests. There were middle-aged white hippies, young sharply dressed African Americans, a healthy selection of New York hipsters, and even one elderly woman with a walker. Because of the theme's party, many of them were holding or wearing flowers.

While we waited to depart, I chatted with Jacob's sister, whom I hadn't seen in a while. Zvia was a few years younger than Jacob, and was finishing up a master's degree at a top U.S. university. Although she'd visited Jacob in Israel a good number of times, she'd never lived there, and had no plans to.

"Maybe I'd visit for a few months—at the most," she said. "It's hard to get around. The people are not helpful, and abrasive. I don't like Middle Eastern food, and I don't think Israeli men are attractive."

I laughed. I always forgot how cutting Zvia could be.

"What did you think when Jacob went off there?" I asked her.

"I thought that he moved there because he didn't want to pay rent in New York," she answered. "And I'm still pretty sure that's the real reason why he went. Not his supposed 'Zionist dream.'"

She then went on to say that she had been surprised by how long he had been there—five and a half years at that point—but that she still thought that when Jacob and Nicole had kids they would come home to New York.

"It must be scary to raise kids there," she said.

I'd once had a conversation with a U.S. State Department Foreign Service trainee about that subject. She had been visiting Israel when I'd been living there, and the two of us had been sitting on the beach in Tel Aviv, when a young Israeli woman and her two small children had appeared in front of us and begun playing at the shore. One of the kids splashed the other, and they both laughed. The mother watched them and smiled.

And Lauren, my Foreign Service trainee friend, said, "If I were an Israeli or Palestinian woman, I wouldn't have kids. There's no point."

The ride to Sir Ivan's estate seemed to take forever. I'd never been so far out on Long Island before, and the idea of having to travel all the way back a few hours later was daunting.

"I wonder what time we're going back," Nicole said.

"Hopefully very soon," I said, already exhausted.

And then we saw it. A castle. An honest-to-God castle—and, somehow, I got a burst of energy.

I guess I sort of expected it to have been a big house, or even a sprawling mansion. Not an actual castle, with towers, a moat, and a drawbridge—and, we'd been told on our way there, a torture chamber. But that's what it was. A castle, towering out of the green Hamptons landscape. No one else I knew had one of those.

As we got off the bus, there were security guards in suits waiting for us, as well as what seemed like a lot of people taking our photos. Most of the party was held behind the castle, where there was a large pool, surrounded by flowers and little bonfires and blanketed by smoke from a smoke machine. Along with all that, for a few minutes after we arrived, the whole place was awash in a pulsing strobe light that seemed designed to cause an epileptic seizure.

"That's totally going to make someone fall into the pool and drown," Zvia said.

The castle itself looked down at us all, a huge flag draped over its side. It was an American flag, except instead of the stars there was a peace sign, and overlayed on top of the stripes, in large letters, were the words "Sir Ivan." I wondered if this sign was always there, or if it had been put up just for the occasion.

Staring at the peace sign on the flag, I thought about my own peacemaking quest. Was this what I was missing? A giant castle? A huge flag? Billions of dollars? Possibly.

There were mats, pillows, and even actual beds arrayed around the pool, and we found a place to sit in a corner, on a large bed that looked like it could have come from somebody's bedroom. On it, as on many of the other beds and mats, was for no apparent reason an enormous stuffed rabbit. I leaned back on it, and tried to get a sense of who the other people at this event were. They ranged in age from about twenty-one to eighty, and they wore all manner of dress, from formal to full-out hippie garb.

But for a long time there was no sign of Sir Ivan himself.

Only when the grounds had filled up with the roughly four-hundred attendees, and all of them were a couple of drinks in, did we get the first sighting of the man himself.

"That must be him," I heard someone nearby say.

"Sir Ivan," someone else said in a whisper—which was unnecessary, since nobody was going to hear over the music and the noise of the crowd.

But I didn't see him and wasn't sure where everyone was looking.

"That's Sir Ivan," someone else said, and beside me, Abby figured out where he was and pointed for me.

Sir Ivan was above us. He was standing on the castle's main balcony, gripping the railing and staring out into the distance as if it didn't even cross his mind that there were a few hundred increasingly intoxicated strangers milling around in his backyard. He stood there in a way that seemed to invite all of us to look up at him while he surveyed his kingdom. He was in his fifties, I estimated, older than I had expected.

Also: Sir Ivan was wearing a cape.

I thought I was seeing things at first, but there was no mistaking it. As he stood up there, gazing out, a full-scale cape billowed out behind him in the breeze.

"If you can't wear a cape at your own party," Luke said, "then you can never wear one."

Abby nodded and said, "If I threw a party like this, I'd wear a cape too."

I looked at her and frowned. I didn't like that image at all.

"I'm sure his Holocaust-surviving father would love all this," Zvia said.

A few seconds later Sir Ivan turned and strode back into the castle, his cape blowing out behind him. I went to get myself another drink, and by the time I was back, reclining on the huge stuffed rabbit, Sir Ivan had returned to the balcony and was gazing out again. This time another guy was with him. They seemed to be discussing something. The second man was not wearing a cape.

I wondered about this other guy. Was he an advisor? A friend? What was his role in the efforts of the Peaceman? And how did he get to this place in life? What path did you have to take to end up hanging out with the cape-wearing Sir Ivan on his castle balcony, while the rest of us plebes looked up at you?

Meanwhile, Luke and Zvia had gone off to find the restrooms in the castle and had come back with some pretty astonishing news.

"Sir Ivan has an entire room full of stuffed rabbits," Luke said. "An entire room."

I looked at the white rabbit I was leaning up against, and at the others scattered about the grounds, and tried to picture a whole room full of them.

"Let me just stress," Zvia said, "that these are *different* stuffed rabbits than the ones out here. These ones are his party rabbits, I guess. Those are for other occasions."

"I think it's pretty unfair," Luke added, "that he has a whole room just for them. I don't even have a whole room just for my living room. It has to share the space with my kitchen."

Maybe it was because of this slap in the face that Luke started to up his drinking at the party. I found this a bit concerning, given his prior history. He was one of those people who seemed totally sober for most of the evening, and then when he suddenly crossed a line, it was like a switch had been flipped from "charming and sober" to "dangerously crazy," and then anything at all could happen. So, as Luke continued to drink at Sir Ivan's, I started to worry that he might flip that switch and do something that would land us in Sir Ivan's torture chamber.

When it did happen, we were both leaning on the stuffed rabbit, watching a half-naked man and a half-naked woman in the pool have exhibitionist half sex, and I was discussing my peace project with him.

"Maybe I've just been wasting my time," I said, "or everyone's time. I don't know what I thought I was doing."

He gave me a sympathetic smile, while two men just near us went up to one of the little bonfires and tried to use it to light cigars.

"That's a bad idea," I said.

"Yes, it is," Luke said. "Yes, it is."

I told him some details about my latest trip to Washington. About how both Nabil Abuznaid, the Palestinian, and Meyrav Wurmser, the Israeli, seemed ready to throw up their hands with regard to the whole situation. I told him about the AIPAC building and the small offices of J-Street—and about how M. J. Rosenberg had said the AIPAC building was built as a message to the DC community. I also mentioned how he had called my hair "adorable." I even admitted to dancing with Meredith at the CUFI, but stressed that it hadn't made me feel any closer to the Lord.

In retrospect, I told Luke, I had become aware that during the course of my whole project, I had spoken to far more people on the Jewish and Zionist side of the spectrum than on the Palestinian side. This was a serious flaw, and I felt bad about it. Maybe it had been my undoing.

I also complained that none of what I had done had really led anywhere. Although I had heard opinions from all over the spectrum, I hadn't made any real progress. As my journey was coming to a close, I didn't have a whole lot to show for it, except the Christians United for Israel tote bag, the PeaceMaker boxer shorts, and the Jewish Defense League T-shirt. And some new friends and, probably, some new enemies too.

But no peace, and no signs of it on the horizon either.

I had still had no luck connecting properly with Kevin at the White House. And Bill Clinton, Jimmy Carter, Henry Kissinger, and most of the other big shots had never gotten back to me at all.

"They probably get these kinds of requests all the time," Luke said.

"Yeah," I said, "from other people trying to make peace."

"But you know," he went on, "the more you do this stuff, the more you continue it—even after your book is done—the more access you'll probably get, and the deeper you'll get into that whole world."

I nodded and smiled. I was grateful for his encouragement, but the fact was that I didn't really want to continue with it, and definitely didn't want to get deeper "into that whole world." The main reason I had begun this project was that I was tired of the whole debate and all the people involved. In the long run, I wasn't interested in getting deeper into it at all. I was interested in getting out. But in the short term, I had been hoping to make some progress toward peace.

Maybe it was the wine I was sipping, or the general atmosphere of absurdity around us, but I started telling him about my PeaceMaker underwear, and wondering aloud if it would have helped anything if the people in DC had known I was wearing it.

Suddenly a waft of marijuana smoke drifted by—and that was when it happened. That was when Luke passed the switch-flipping point. He looked at me, now unfocused, and then mumbled something about how I should stop talking about my underwear so much. I could see in his eyes that we had lost him for the night.

Then, sniffing at the air as the marijuana scent faded away, he said, "I'll be right back."

And that was pretty much it for Luke. He had passed the point of no return, and although I saw him periodically as the party progressed, he was never even vaguely coherent again.

A little later we were ushered into the castle itself. Without being told what was about to happen, we were directed into a large room on the ground floor that had a built-in stage on one side and large speakers on the other.

"The guy has black lights permanently set up in his house," Abby said, pointing at the ceiling.

That was true, and as a result of the black lights, we were all glowing, as the next part of the evening's festivities began. Squeezed into that performance space, glowing and bathed in threads of smoke from a smoke machine, while outside half-naked models lounged beside huge stuffed rabbits, we may have thought we knew what weirdness was. But really, the weirdness had only just begun.

Because now Sir Ivan stormed onstage. He was wearing a different cape now, a more flamboyant one—bedecked with a peace sign. This was clearly his performance cape.

Then the music started up, and Sir Ivan began dancing wildly on stage, flinging his arms around, and making aggressively animated facial expressions, while two female backup dancers gyrated on either side of him. The song was a fast dance-music remix of "Kumbaya."

"Kumbaya," he sang. "Kumbaya."

And then: "Kumbaya! Give them love!"

As far as I could tell, these were the only words in his loud, frenetic version of the song—just shouted out at increasingly manic volume and speed.

When the song reached a particularly up-tempo part, Sir Ivan suddenly produced two bright glow sticks and held them out in front of him. Then he upped his dancing a few notches in intensity, and I started to think he might collapse or have a heart attack.

"Kumbaya!" he shouted again. "Give them love!"

It was beginning to feel like I was in some kind of cult. I looked around the crowd, curious as to what my fellow attendees were doing and thinking. After all, I thought, we were all subject to Sir Ivan's whims at this point. We had no way to get back to New York City without his buses—I didn't even really know *where* we were in the Hamptons—and the caped figure prancing around on stage, with his purported torture chamber presumably nearby, seemed capable of just about anything.

But when he finished his energetic techno version of "Kumbaya" it looked like Sir Ivan was about to pass out from exhaustion, and he just flopped offstage and disappeared. Those two minutes were his whole performance, and we were now led back out into the castle grounds.

After that, Sir Ivan was absent for a while, and I figured he was recovering. When he finally did reappear later, he was wearing yet another cape. This one was a little more subdued than either of his two earlier ones.

"Now *that's* a guy with a lot of different capes," Jacob said.

At the end of the night, when it was finally time to get on the buses back to Manhattan, we were all pretty grateful. It had been a night to remember, but at a certain point Sir Ivan's hospitality began to tire us all out.

Zvia said that she wanted to take one of the big stuffed rabbits home with her, but there were people leaning on the one near us, so she didn't. This turned out to be a wise decision; as we left, another girl walked quickly ahead of us, carrying one of the rabbits, and one of Sir Ivan's burly suit-wearing security guards yelled out, "We have to rescue the bunny!"

Apparently, even though Sir Ivan—the "Peaceman"—was so full of love and kindness that he felt the need to share it with the world, he was pretty possessive of his stuffed rabbits.

My friends and I stood there in astonishment as half a dozen of the security guards ran after the girl with the rabbit, and were then followed by a black SUV. I didn't see what happened, but

248

none of us saw that girl or the stolen rabbit again. She may still be in Sir Ivan's torture chamber.

We were handed gift bags and wearily got on the bus. On the drive home, I sat beside Abby, and the others in our group sat farther behind. And very soon after departing from outside the castle, the bus was more or less silent. Most people were sleeping, or pondering the night we had had.

"I feel dirty from this experience," Abby said, and fell asleep beside me.

I looked in my gift bag, and found a neon green pillow with a peace sign on it and a CD that had several different versions of Sir Ivan's rendition of "Kumbaya."

Excellent, I thought. *Excellent.*

I lay back on the pillow and closed my eyes. Everything was quiet as we shot through the Hamptons darkness.

Except for one thing. The silence was pierced at one point by what was unmistakably Luke's drunken voice from the back of the bus.

"Jacob is my best friend," he shouted out in a singsongy tune, for no apparent reason. (The next day I would hear that during the bus ride, he had inexplicably removed his pants.) And then things were quiet again.

But I couldn't sleep. Something about the night had put me in a reflective mood, and my mind was flooded by images and words from the preceding months.

Had I learned anything from it all? Was I any closer to understanding what was needed to create peace? Was it time for me to get my own cape?

*   *   *

Back in my apartment, I had to consider the sad fact that I was more or less finished with my attempts to broker peace, and the reality was that there was not yet peace in the Middle East.

I thought about this while I put on Sir Ivan's CD, and listened to him sing his various "Kumbaya" remixes. On one of them he had a recording of Barack Obama giving an inspirational speech in the background, while Sir Ivan sang "Kumbaya" overtop of it.

"Enough," Abby told me eventually, "I can't listen to that anymore. The whole thing is so creepy. I just want to forget that we were even there."

Indeed, while I had planned to take the neon peace sign–decorated pillows home with us along with the CD, Abby had made me leave them behind.

"I don't want those things in my house," she had said.

But when she was off at work—Abby had a new job, where unlike me, she was doing something obviously productive—I put the CD back on. Listening to it, and wearing my PeaceMaker boxer shorts, I turned on my computer and booted up the Peace-Maker simulator.

Choosing to play the side of the Israeli prime minister again, I tried to plug in the policies and ideas my various advisors had advocated to me. The all-out war of Daniel Pipes, the JDL, and Ted Collins. The dovishness of Samar Assad and my friend P.J. AIPAC's right of center approach. J-Street's left of center approach. And combinations thereof.

I made endless concessions to the Palestinians. I waged war

against the Palestinians. I tried to walk some middle ground. But nothing worked. Either I started the "Third Intifada" again, or the Israeli populace voted me out of office. Apparently, in the months I'd been peacemaking, I had learned absolutely nothing.

Reluctantly, I shut off the game.

I left the apartment and, singing Sir Ivan's "Kumbaya" under my breath, I walked down the street to the fruit stand.

"Kumbaya," I mumbled. "Kumbaya! Give them love!"

But when I got to the stand, I found that my grocer wasn't there. Instead, an old woman was standing behind the counter.

"That guy who works here . . ." I said, proceeding to describe him.

"Yes," she said.

"Do you know if he is going to be in today?"

She shook her head.

"He won't be here anymore," she told me.

"What?" I asked. "What do you mean?"

"He went West," she said, "to work on the highways."

He had apparently been serious when he told me about his plan to go West. I still didn't really know what this meant for him, but I knew what it meant for me. As I closed off my project, I wouldn't be able to discuss it with him, or tell him how it had all ended. I wouldn't be able to ask him if I had been wasting my time or if I had been doing something worthwhile.

"Thanks," I said to the old woman, and walked off.

The grocer was looking westward, I thought, while I had still been trapped looking East. He had managed to firmly escape the Middle East and its power, and now I would have to do the same.

I got back to my apartment and sat down at my desk. Over the past few months, I'd come to question a lot of my assumptions about the Middle East situation, but I hadn't really found any answers. In a sense, the way to fix the situation seemed pretty obvious. Divide the land into two states, split Jerusalem fairly, remove the bulk of the settlements, and have the Palestinians renounce any further claims.

The real trick was getting there, without the extremists on both sides—who basically seemed to share the same goal: endless war—torpedoing the whole thing.

Absently, I checked my email and voice mail for some word from Kevin at the White House. But there was none. Wherever it was "overseas" that he had been heading to when he had called me, maybe he hadn't yet returned.

It was sadly perfect, I thought, that I had never been able to connect properly with Kevin or his White House colleagues. Firstly, of course, even after all my exploration, I wouldn't really have known what advice to give to Kevin to pass along to the president. If I had tried, it probably would have been incoherent and involved stuffed bunnies.

But it also felt sort of symbolic that I hadn't been able to connect with the White House. Even if I had come up with a real peace plan, apparently, I wouldn't have been able to give it to the people who mattered most. As Meyrav Wurmser had told me, the idea of peace was just a temptress.

In any case, I knew I couldn't continue trying to reach Kevin. My project had run its course and, let's be honest: I now had to sit down and write this book about it.

*   *   *

As I did that, Kevin's boss, the president, was working with a Middle East mired in tragedy and continually teetering on the edge of outright catastrophe. At the new opening session of the UN's General Assembly, he made a speech calling on both sides to step up to the peacemaking plate, and facilitated a short, unproductive meeting between the Israeli and Palestinian leaders.

There were an increasing number of rumors and predictions that the lack of movement on the peace front was on the verge of causing a third Palestinian Intifada. All it needed, some were saying, was an inciting incident. A spark. But since the Israel-Iran situation threatened to itself ignite the region at any moment, the Netanyahu government seemed to have little time or willingness to devote its energy to the Palestinian track.

Some of the Palestinian leadership, meanwhile, appeared to have lost patience—just like their representative in DC had. Mahmoud Abbas, the Palestinian president, was threatening not to run for reelection and to walk away from it all. And Palestinian prime minister Salam Fayyad was reportedly considering doing an end run around the "peace process" by simply declaring a Palestinian state. There were even reports that the Obama White House might be considering supporting this move and, that hearing this, Israel was sending nervous messages to the U.S. to reconsider.

Even Thomas Friedman of the *New York Times* wrote a piece advocating an American disengagement from the peacemaking game.

How to Make Peace in the Middle East

"Take down our 'Peace-Processing-Is-Us' sign and just go home," he wrote. "If we are still begging Israel to stop building settlements, which is so manifestly idiotic, and the Palestinians to come to negotiations, which is so manifestly in their interest, and the Saudis to just give Israel a wink, which is so manifestly pathetic, we are in the wrong place. It's time to call a halt to this dysfunctional 'peace process.'"

I thought that there was definitely something to this but couldn't help thinking that just giving up would be a tremendous betrayal of all the Israeli children who wanted to live a life free of the constant fear of terrorism, and of all the Palestinian children who were suffering from hunger, a lack of medical supplies, and the threat of being caught in the crossfire once again.

Didn't we owe them more?

Meanwhile, Ray Hanania, the Palestinian standup comedian I had spoken with, suddenly announced that he was going to run for president of Palestine. He didn't have much of a chance of winning, of course, but I knew that his campaign was only somewhat tongue-in-cheek. He had conciliatory, moderate ideas he would have liked to implement, and unlike almost everyone else, he seemed to somehow be able to remain resolutely optimistic about the prospects for peace. I emailed him to congratulate him on his campaign, and he thanked me. Then he told me that he was forming a council of advisors and, to my surprise, he even invited me to be one of them.

And despite what seemed like a groundswell of people giving up on peacemaking, J-Street's first national conference went well, with more than 1,500 attendees and nearly 150 members of Congress present. The Obama administration even sent General James Jones, the national security advisor, to provide the keynote address, confirming that the pro-peace movement might be ascendant.

I wrote to Shmuel Rosner, long-time DC bureau chief for Israel's liberal *Haaretz* newspaper, who had recently moved to the more conservative *Jerusalem Post,* asking him what he thought of the changes that seemed to be afoot in Washington's Middle East dynamics.

"Americans," he wrote back, "have to understand that Israel is a real country with real concerns and needs—that has to make real decisions. And that such decisions can't always be in line with the liberal agenda and the noble intentions and tendencies of supporters who live comfortably and enjoy the luxury of being comfortably protected by the might of the greatest empire in the history of the world."

Indeed, as if agreeing with Rosner's analysis, the Israeli ambassador pointedly skipped J-Street's conference, and the Israeli Embassy issued a statement saying that some of J-Street's dovish policies could "impair Israel's interests."

Maybe, I thought, *Thomas Friedman is right.*

There was one sliver of good news for me, personally.

Out of the blue one day, while I was trying to craft everything I had experienced into this book, my uncle called me. As we talked, I discovered that when he had spoken angrily to me on the phone before, he had apparently not yet even read my first book. On this call, his voice sounded starkly different.

"Now that I've read your first book," he told me, "I understand it more. You were trying to show that everyone involved in the conflict are just humans, right? With all the stupid and silly things that humans do?"

"I think so," I said. "That, and to make readers laugh."

"That's good," he said, "because with the giant mess over there, and all the suffering—which isn't going to stop—maybe that's all we can do in the end."

After we said good-bye and hung up, I found that I was smiling, but I wasn't sure if I was happy or sad. The conflict in the Middle East wasn't going anywhere, I knew, but I would now at least be able to tell Abby that I was ready to stop playing my "little games," as she had put it.

If I couldn't make peace in the Middle East, I thought, at least I could try to make peace with the Middle East.

Acknowledgments

I'd like to offer my thanks to everyone who appears in this book, as well as those who were equally generous with their help, but who didn't end up in the final version of the manuscript. Even if I didn't manage to fit in your specific words, your thoughts definitely aided me a great deal.

I'd also like to express my profound gratitude to:

Everyone at Free Press and Simon & Schuster for giving me the opportunity to write another book, and for the work they've put into it: Martha K. Levin, Dominick V. Anfuso, Leah Miller, Sydney Tanigawa, and, most of all, my editor, Wylie O'Sullivan.

The team at Foundry Literary + Media, especially my astoundingly good agent, Mollie Glick.

My film agents at the United Talent Agency: Geoff Morley, Yuli Masinovsky, and Howie Sanders.

At Ryerson University, all my colleagues and friends—especially the unmatchable Natasha Flora, and my student assistants, Alona Glikin and Vanessa Giugovaz. At the University of St. Andrews, Meaghan Delahunt, Robert Crawford, and everyone else at the School of English. Thank you for your encouragement and your patience.

For giving me the ridiculously tiny computer on which most of this book was actually written: Dan Stopnicki, Zack Silver, Hanna Badreddine-Silver, Tatyana Kozakova, Bryan Redinger, and Shawna Gutfreund.

For being so supportive of my books and my other writing: Mark Greller, Scott Perraud, Jacob Shwirtz, Andrea Janes, Rebecca Sinderbrand, Joy Sinderbrand, Steve Kastenbaum, memDesigns, The Jewish Book Network, Joseph Braude, Matt Polly, Marni Banack, Mark Svartz, Adam Kushner, Mark Follman, Michael Ross, Rachel Shukert, Evan Handler, Jonathan Kay, Andrew Krucoff, Hilary Krieger, Greg Veis, David Sax, Joshua Landy, Sarah Posner, Nick Wechsler, Elizabeth Bradford, and most especially, David Gerson.

My entire extended family: the Ipps, Dicks, Stones, Leveys, Levines, Cohens, Cooks, and Goldbergs. My sister Simone, brother Ryan, brother-in-law Ari, and my parents.

And without a doubt, most of all, my wife Abby—who, one could safely say, puts up with a lot.

A Note on Permissions

Short sections of this book previously appeared in *Newsweek, Salon, The Jerusalem Report,* and *The Nervous Breakdown.* I am grateful to each of these publications for the permission to reuse them here.

Index

Index

Index

Index

Index

Index

Index

Index

Index

Index

About the Author

GREGORY LEVEY is the author of *Shut Up, I'm Talking: And Other Diplomacy Lessons I Learned in the Israeli Government*. He has written for *Newsweek, The New Republic,* the *New York Post, Salon, The Globe and Mail,* and other publications. He served as a speechwriter and delegate for the Israeli government at the United Nations and as Senior Foreign Communications Coordinator for prime ministers Ariel Sharon and Ehud Olmert, and is now on the faculty of Ryerson University in Toronto, Canada.